german phrasebook
paul stocker

D1385921

For UK order enquiries: please contact Bookpoint Ltd, 130 Milton Park, Abingdon, Oxon OX14 4SB. Telephone: +44 (0)1235 827720. Fax: +44 (0)1235 400454. Lines are open 09.00–18.00, Monday to Saturday, with a 24-hour message answering service. Details about our titles and how to order are available at www.teachyourself.co.uk

For USA order enquiries: please contact McGraw-Hill Customer Services, PO Box 545, Blacklick, OH 43004-0545, USA. Telephone: 1-800-722-4726. Fax: 1-614-755-5645.

For Canada order enquiries: please contact McGraw-Hill Ryerson Ltd, 300 Water St, Whitby, Ontario L1N 9B6, Canada. Telephone: 905 430 5000. Fax: 905 430 5020.

Long renowned as the authoritative source for self-guided learning – with more than 30 million copies sold worldwide – the **teach yourself** series includes over 300 titles in the fields of languages, crafts, hobbies, business, computing and education.

British Library Cataloguing in Publication Data: a catalogue record for this title is available from the British Library.

Library of Congress Catalog Card Number: on file.

First published in UK 2004 by Hodder Arnold, 338 Euston Road, London, NW1 3BH.

First published in US 2005 by Contemporary Books, a division of the McGraw-Hill Companies, 1 Prudential Plaza, 130 East Randolph Street, Chicago, IL 60601 USA.

This edition published 2004.

The **teach yourself** name is a registered trade mark of Hodder Headline Ltd.

Author: Paul Stocker

Text and illustrations © Hodder & Stoughton Educational 2004

Printed and bound in Spain.

Impression number 10 9 8 7 6 5 4 3 2

Year 2010 2009 2008 2007 2006 2005

CONTENTS

③

INTRODUCTION

This *Teach Yourself German Phrasebook* is an essential accessory for travellers of all ages. The main section of the book consists of phrases and sentences organised in a way which will make it easy for you to select the items which will say what YOU want to say.

Start by familiarising yourself with the **Pronunciation Guide** and the **Useful Everyday Phrases**. If you can, practise the phrases you might need beforehand. To help you understand what is being said to you, you will find sections headed *'You may hear'* or *'You may see'* scattered through the book. There is also a **Dictionary** of the most common words and a section of **Essential Information**.

Grammar

German speakers will rarely misunderstand you if you make grammatical mistakes – they will in any case be impressed that you are making an effort to use their language. German is a relatively logical language with few exceptions to its rules. Two short explanations may be useful here:

You German has three words for 'you' to our one. You will notice that all are given in this book, where appropriate. Use as follows:

Sie – polite word for 'you', whether one person or a group; use with anyone you don't know well.

du – informal word for 'you', for just one person; use with a friend, relative, child or animal.

ihr – as for du, but with two or more friends.

In this phrasebook the polite form is denoted by a (P) and the familiar alternative follows in brackets and is denoted by an (F).

The and *a*   English speakers often wonder why there are several words for 'the' and 'a' in German; this is because the basic words **der, die, das** (all of which mean 'the') and **ein, eine** (meaning 'a' or 'an') change their endings according to where they stand in the sentence - rather like 'he' and 'him' or 'they' and 'them' in English.

Gute Reise!

PRONUNCIATION GUIDE

The pronunciation of German is very similar to English and the
pronunciation guide for every phrase will allow you to say the
German with ease; moreover, letters and combinations of letters in
German are always pronounced the same way. The main points to
be aware of are as follows:

SYMBOL		GERMAN		ENGLISH
g	*as in*	gerade	*compare with*	**g**et
kh		Loch*		lo**ch**
kv		Quantität		black **v**elvet
s		das		**s**ay
sh		spielen		**sh**ip
ts		Zimmer		ve**ts**
Y		ja		**y**es

z		sie	rose
a		kann	man
aa		fahren	far
ai		wenig	aim
e		wenn	men
ee		wir	seem
ew		Hügel	*see below*
i		bitte	tin
I }	see	Eis	I
y }	below	leider	fly
o		Woche	not
oh		Person	more
oo		umsteigen	room
ow		laufen	how
oy		heute	boy
ur		möchte	burn

* 'ch' is pronounced 'kh' after a, o, u and au; in all other cases it is pronounced as English 'sh', and is shown as such in this book.

The German letter 'ß' is pronounced 'ss'.

The sound ew (ü) is pronounced as ee, but with the lips rounded as for oo.

The 'y' symbol is generally used to represent the vowel sound in, for example, 'fly'. The 'I' symbol is used at the beginning of words for clarity.

When you see the following letters in written German, they are always pronounced as shown:

sch = *sh*	**v** = f
w = v	**ä** = e or ai
ei = I	**ie** = ee

Stressed syllables are indicated by underlining.

BASIC EXPRESSIONS

THE BASICS

Yes/No	Ja/Nein *Yaa/nyn*
Please/Thank you	Bitte/Danke *bitter/danker*
Excuse me	Entschuldigung *entshooldeegoong*
Can you help me?	Können Sie mir helfen? *kurnen zee meer helfen?*
Good morning/afternoon (evening)	Guten Tag (Abend) *Gooten taag/aabent*
I'm sorry	Es tut mir Leid *Ess toot meer lyt*
Good	Gut *goot*

OK

OK
okay

That's right

Stimmt
Shtimmt

ASKING

Where is ...?

Wo ist ...?
Voh ist ...?

Where can I get ...?

Wo bekomme ich ...?
Voh berkommer ish ...?

How much is it?

Was kostet das?
Vas kostet das?

I'd like ...

Ich möchte ...
ish murshter ...

PROBLEMS, ASKING FOR HELP

I don't know

Ich weiß es nicht
ish vyss ess nisht

Do you speak English?

Sprechen Sie Englisch?
shpreshen zee ennglish?

I (don't) understand

Ich verstehe (nicht)
ish fairshtai-er (nisht)

Do you understand?

Verstehen Sie?
fairshtai-en zee?

Could you speak slower?

Können Sie bitte langsamer
sprechen?
*kurnen zee bitter langsaamer
shpreshen?*

Could you repeat that?

Können Sie das bitte wiederholen?
*kurnen zee dass bitter
veederhohlen?*

What does that mean?

Was bedeutet das?
vas berdoytet das?

Pardon?

Wie bitte?
vee bitter?

Could you translate this for me?	Könnten Sie mir das übersetzen? *k<u>u</u>rnten zee meer das ewberz<u>e</u>tsen?*
Could you write that down?	Können Sie das bitte aufschreiben? *k<u>u</u>rnen zee dass b<u>i</u>tter <u>ow</u>f-shryben?*
I can't speak (much) German	Ich spreche kein/wenig Deutsch *ish spr<u>e</u>sher kyn/w<u>ai</u>nig doych*
I've lost my way	Ich habe mich verlaufen *ish h<u>aa</u>ber mish fairl<u>ow</u>fen*
Where is the British/American Embassy/Consulate?	Wo ist die britische/ amerikanische Botschaft/das Konsulat? *voh ist dee br<u>i</u>tisher/amerik<u>aa</u>nisher b<u>oh</u>tshaft/ das konzool<u>aa</u>t?*

GREETINGS AND MAKING FRIENDS

Meeting people

Two sorts of phrases are provided here:

The first, marked **P** (= Polite) uses the more formal word for 'you' (*Sie*); adults talking to adults, or young people talking to adults they don't know, should use this list initially.

The second, marked **F** (= Familiar), uses the familiar *du* for 'you', and is used by teenagers, and by friends of any age.

Good morning	Guten Morgen *g<u>oo</u>ten m<u>o</u>rgen*
Good afternoon	Guten Tag *g<u>oo</u>ten taag*

It's not difficult to make friends in Germany.
It will be especially appreciated if you try to do so in German!

Good evening	Guten Abend _gooten aabent_
Goodbye (in person)	Auf Wiedersehen _owf veederzai-en_
(on phone)	Auf Wiederhören _owf veederhuren_
Bye!	Tschüs! _chewss!_
What's your name?	(P) Wie heißen Sie? _vee hysen zee?_
	(F) Wie heißt du? _vee hyst doo?_
My name is ...	Ich heiße ... _ish hyser ..._
How are you?	(P) Wie geht es Ihnen? _vee gait es eenen?_
	(F) Wie geht's? _vee gaits?_
Fine, thanks. And you?	(P) Gut, danke. Und Ihnen? _goot, danker. oont eenen?_
	(F) Gut, danke. Und dir? _goot, danker. oont deer?_
Pleased to meet you	Freut mich _froyt mish_
Where are you staying at the moment?	(P) Wo wohnen Sie zur Zeit? _voh vohnen zee tsoor tsyt?_
	(F) Wo wohnst du zur Zeit? _voh vohnst doo tsoor tsyt?_
I'm staying...	Ich wohne... _ish vohner..._
Where do you come from?	(P) Woher kommen Sie? _voh-hair kommen zee?_
	(F) Woher kommst du? _voh-hair kommst doo?_

I'm from...	Ich komme aus... *ish kommer ows...*
...America	...Amerika *amerika*
...Australia	...Australien *owstraalien*
...Britain	...Großbritannien *grohs-britaanien*
...Canada	...Kanada *kanada*
...Ireland	...Irland *eerlant*
...Scotland	...Schottland *shotlant*
...Wales	...Wales *vaylz*
I'm a businessman/ businesswoman	Ich bin Geschäftsmann/ Geschäftsfrau *ish bin gersheftsmann/ gersheftsfrow*
I'm a student	Ich bin Student *ish bin shtoodent*
I'm on holiday	Ich bin auf Urlaub *ish bin owf oorlowp*
I'm single/married/divorced	Ich bin verheiratet/ledig/ geschieden *ish bin fairhyrartert/laidig/ gersheeden*
I (don't) like playing tennis	Ich spiele (nicht) gern Tennis *ish shpeeler (nisht) gairn tennis*
Do you like it here?	(P) Gefällt es Ihnen hier? *gerfelt es eenen heer?*
	(F) Gefällt es dir hier? *gerfelt es deer heer?*

Are you here on holiday?	(P) Sind Sie auf Urlaub hier? *zint zee owf oorlowp heer?*
	(F) Bist du auf Urlaub hier? *bist doo owf oorlowp heer?*
I'm on a business trip	Ich bin auf Geschäftsreise *ish bin owf gersheftsryzer*
I work for...	Ich arbeite bei... *ish aarbyter by...*
Are you on your own?	(P) Sind Sie allein? *zint zee alyn?*
	(F) Bist du allein? *bist doo alyn?*
My ... is/are here too	... ist/sind auch hier *ist/zint owkh heer*
...boyfriend	Mein Freund... *myn froynt...*
...brother	Mein Bruder... *myn brooder...*
...family	Meine Familie... *myner fameeli-er...*
...father	Mein Vater... *myn faater...*
...girlfriend	Meine Freundin... *myner froyndin...*
...husband	Mein Mann... *myn man...*
...mother	Meine Mutter... *myner mooter...*
...parents	Meine Eltern... *myner eltern...*
...sister	Meine Schwester... *myner shvester...*

...wife	Meine Frau... *myner frow...*
Do you have a light please?	(P) Haben Sie Feuer, bitte? *haaben zee foyer, bitter?* (F) Hast du Feuer, bitte? *hast doo foyer, bitter?*
Would you like a cigarette?	(P) Möchten Sie eine Zigarette? *murshten zee I-ner tsigaretter?* (F) Möchtest du eine Zigarette? *murshtest doo I-ner tsigaretter?*
I'm afraid I don't/haven't	Leider nicht *lyder nisht*
Would you like a drink?	(P) Möchten Sie etwas trinken? *murshten zee etvas trinken?* (F) Möchtest du etwas trinken? *murshtest doo etvas trinken?*
I'd like	ich möchte... *ish murshter...*
Nothing for me, thanks	Nichts für mich, danke *nishts fewr mish, danker*
Cheers!	Prost! *prohst!*

AT RECEPTION

My name is...	Ich heiße... *ish hysser...*
I have an appointment with Mr./Ms. ...	Ich habe eine Verabredung mit Herrn/Frau ... *ish haaber I-ner* *fairapraidoong mit* *hairn/frow ...*

I'd like to see Mr/Ms ...	Ich möchte Herrn/Frau ... sprechen *ish murshter hairn/frow ... sphreshen*

You may hear:

Vorsicht! *fohrzisht!*	Careful! Watch out!
Bitte schön? *bitter shurn?*	May I help you?
Bitte schön *bitter shurn*	Here you are/you're welcome
Moment, bitte. *moment, bitter*	Wait a moment, please
Danke, gleichfalls *danker, glyshfalls*	And the same to you
Ich bin hier fremd *ish bin heer fremt*	I'm a stranger here

SIGNS AND NOTICES

Ausfahrt	Exit (vehicles)
Aufzug	Lift
Ausgang	Exit
Auskunft	Information
außer ...	except for ...
Außer Betrieb	Out of order
Belegt	No vacancies
Besetzt	Occupied
Bitte nicht stören	Do not disturb
Damen	Ladies
Drücken	Push
Einfahrt	Entrance (vehicles)

In German, the title for all adult women, married or single, is *Frau*. *Fräulein* is rarely used.

Eingang	Entrance
Eintritt frei	Entrance fee
Erdgeschoss	ground floor
Feiertag	public holiday
Fußgänger	pedestrians
Gefahr	Danger
Geschlossen	Closed
Heiß	Hot
Herren	Men
Kalt	Cold
Kasse	Till/cash desk
Kein Zutritt	No entry
nicht …	do not …
Nicht berühren	Do not touch
Nicht rauchen	no smoking
Notausgang	Emergency exit
Notruf	Emergency phone
nur …	… only
Öffnungszeiten	hours of opening
Rauchen verboten	No smoking
Selbstbedienung	Self-service
Stammtisch	Table reserved for regular customers
Stock	floor, storey
Tiefgeschoss	basement
Ziehen	Pull
Zimmer frei	Vacancies
Zu verkaufen	For sale
Zu vermieten	For hire/rent

Are you waiting for someone?	(P) Warten Sie auf jemanden? *vaarten zee owf yaimanden?*
	(F) Wartest du auf jemanden? *vaartest doo owf yaimanden?*
Are you free this evening?	(P) Haben Sie heute Abend Zeit? *haaben zee hoyter aabent tsyt?*
	(F) Hast du heute Abend Zeit? *hast doo hoyter aabent tsyt?*
I'm sorry, I'm not	Leider nicht *lyder nisht*
How about tomorrow?	Und morgen? *oont morgen?*
Would you like to go to a club?	(P) Möchten Sie in eine Disko gehen? *murshten zee in I-ner disko gai-en?*
	(F) Möchtest du in eine Disko gehen? *murshtest doo in I-ner disko gai-en?*
Would you like to come with me/us?	(P) Kommen Sie mit? *kommen zee mit?*
	(F) Kommst du mit? *koomst doo mit?*
Would you like to go for a drink?	(P) Möchten Sie etwas trinken gehen? *murshten zee etvas trinken gai-en?*
	(F) Möchtest du etwas trinken gehen? *murshtest doo etvas trinken gai-en?*

Yes, I would	Ja, gerne *Yaa, gairner*
I'd rather...	Ich würde lieber... *ish vewrder leeber...*
Where shall we meet?	Wo treffen wir uns? *voh treffen veer oons?*
At what time?	Um wie viel Uhr? *oom veefeel oor?*
I'll pick you up	(P) Ich hole Sie ab *ish hohler zee ab* (F) Ich hole dich ab *ish hohler dish ab*
What is your address/phone number?	(P) Wie ist Ihre Adresse/Telefonnummer? *vee ist eerer adresser/telefohn-noomer?* (F) Wie ist deine Adresse/Telefonnummer? *vee ist dyner adresser/telefohn-noomer?*
Would you like to come over?	(P) Möchten Sie zu uns kommen? *murshten ze tsoo oons kommen?* (F) Möchtest du zu uns kommen? *murshtest doo tsoo oons kommen?*

ARRIVAL AND DEPARTURE

- This section deals with arriving and departing in German-speaking countries. For information on travel (by air, or by public transport), see page 50, taxis and car hire pages 62–64.

- See also buying tickets, page 50.

- Watch out for the following differences in place names:

  Basle = Basel
  Black Forest = Schwarzwald
  Cologne = Köln
  Geneva = Genf
  Lake Constance = Bodensee

Munich = München
Nuremburg = Nürnberg
Vienna = Wien
River Rhine = der Rhein
River Danube = die Donau
Baltic Sea = die Ostsee
The Channel = der Kanal
Bavaria = Bayern

Names of other towns in German-speaking countries are spelt similarly in both English and German.

PASSPORT CONTROL

I'm here on business	Ich bin geschäftlich hier *ish bin ger__sheft__lish heer*
We're here on holiday	Wir sind auf Urlaub hier *veer zint owf __oor__lowp heer*
I'm/we're staying...	Ich bleibe/wir bleiben... *ish bl__y__ber/veer bl__y__ben...*
...for 2 days	...zwei Tage *tsvy t__aa__ger*
...for 1 week/2 weeks	...eine Woche/zwei Wochen *__I__-ner __vo__kher/tsvy __vo__khen*
...for 1 month/2 months	...einen Monat/zwei Monate *__I__-nern m__oh__naat/tsvy m__oh__naater*
...till...	...bis zum... *...bis tsoom...*

• See page 158 for dates

We're going...	Wir fahren... *veer f__aa__ren...*
...to the Alps	...in die Alpen *in dee __a__lpen*

...to Austria	...nach Österreich *nakh ursterykh*
...to Germany	...nach Deutschland *nakh doychlant*
...to Switzerland	...in die Schweiz *in dee shvyts*

CUSTOMS

• If you have something to declare, go through the red exit (Anmeldepflichtige Waren); otherwise choose the green exit (Anmeldefreie Waren).

I've nothing to declare	Ich habe nichts zu verzollen *ish haaber nishts tsoo fairtsolen*
Do I have to declare this?	Muss ich das verzollen? *moos ish das fairtsolen?*
How much do I have to pay?	Wie viel muss ich zahlen? *veefeel moos ish tsaalen?*
I've got...	Ich habe... *ish haaber...*
...cigarettes	...Zigaretten *tsigareten*
...cigars	...Zigarren *tsigaren*
...tobacco	...Tabak *tabak*
...spirits	...Spirituosen *shpiritoo-ohzen*
...wine	...Wein *vyn*
...perfume	...Parfüm *parfung*
Here's the receipt	Hier ist die Quittung *heer ist dee kvittoong*

It's a present	Es ist ein Geschenk *es ist I-n gershenk*
Here's my ticket	Hier ist meine Fahrkarte *heer ist myner faarkaarter*
My name is...	Ich heiße... *ish hysser...*
My flight number is...	Meine Flugnummer ist... *myner floognummer ist...*
Here's my address...	Hier ist meine Adresse... *heer ist myner adresser...*

You may hear:

Ihren Pass bitte *eeren pass bitter*	Your passport, please
Wohin fahren Sie? *voh-hin faaren zee?*	Where are you travelling to?
Wie lange bleiben Sie? *vee langer blyben zee?*	How long are you staying?
Bitte öffnen Sie... *bitter urfnen zee...*	Please open...
Haben Sie etwas zu verzollen? *haaben zee etvas tsoo fairtsollen?*	Do you have anything to declare?
Dies ist zollpflichtig *deez ist tsollpflishtig*	You must pay duty on this

You may see:

Abfahrt	Departures
Ankunft	Arrivals
Fluggäste/Passagiere	Passengers
Fluglinie	Airline
Gepäckausgabe	Luggage reclaim
Inland	Internal (flights)
Passkontrolle	Passport control

Zoll	**Customs**
Zollfreie Waren	**Duty-free shop**

LUGGAGE

Where are the luggage trolleys?
Wo sind die Kofferkulis?
voh zint dee koffer-kooliz?

Where do we collect our luggage?
Wo holen wir unser Gepäck ab?
voh hohlen veer oonzer gerpek ap?

Where's the information desk?
Wo ist die Auskunft?
voh ist dee owskoonft?

There's a bag/case missing
Eine Tasche/Ein Koffer fehlt
I-ner tascher/I-n koffer failt

My luggage hasn't arrived yet
Mein Gepäck ist noch nicht da
myn gerpek ist nokh nisht daa

I can't find my luggage
Ich finde mein Gepäck nicht
ish finder myn gerpek nisht

Has the luggage from the London flight arrived yet?
Ist das Gepäck von dem Flug aus London schon da?
ist das gerpek fon daim floog ows london shohn daa?

When will my luggage arrive?
Wann kommt mein Gepäck?
van kommt myn gerpek?

Could you please find out where my luggage is?
Können Sie bitte herausfinden, wo mein Gepäck ist?
kurnen zee bitter herowsfinden, voh myn gerpek ist?

I'm leaving for ... tomorrow/ in two days' time
Ich fahre morgen/in zwei Tagen nach ...
ish faarer morgen/in tsvy taagen nakh...

• Airports and railway stations have luggage trolleys (*Kofferkulis*), for which a small sum may be payable.

DEPARTURE

Here is my ticket/boarding card	Hier ist meine Fahrkarte/meine Bordkarte *heer ist myner faarkaarter/myner bordkaarter*
Can I take this on board?	Kann ich das mit an Bord nehmen? *kan ish das mit an bord naimen?*
How much must I pay for the excess?	Was muss ich für das Übergewicht zahlen? *vas moos ish fewr das ewbergervikht tsaalen?*
From which gate does our flight leave?	Von welchem Flugsteig fährt unser Flug? *fon velshem floogshtyg fairt oonzer floog?*
Has flight (BA960) been called?	Wurde Flug (BA960) schon aufgerufen? *voorder floog (bai aa noyn zekhs nool) shohn owfgeroofen?*
Can I book a seat on another/ the next flight?	Kann ich einen Platz für einen anderen Flug/den nächsten Flug reservieren? *kan ish I-nen plats fewr I-nen anderen floog/dain neshsten floog rezairveeren?*
I've missed my...	Ich habe ... verpasst *ish haabe...fairpasst*
...plane	...meinen Flug... *mynen floog*

...connection	...meinen Anschluss... *mynen anshlooss...*
...coach/bus	...meinen Bus... *mynen boos*
...train	...meinen Zug... *mynen tsoog*
...ferry	...meine Fähre... *myner fairer*

You may hear:

Der Flug nach...hat... Minuten Verspätung *dair floog nakh...hat...* *minooten fairshpaitoong*	The flight to...will be... minutes late

ACCOMMODATION

HOTELS AND YOUTH HOSTELS

* *Zimmer frei* indicates that there are vacancies. *Belegt* or *Besetzt* indicates that all the rooms are taken.

* The choice of accommodation is usually between the following:

Hotel (garni)	**hotel (bed and breakfast)**
Gasthaus/Gasthof	**inn**

If you have not made a booking before your arrival, there are several ways of finding a room. Look out for: *Zimmernachweis* or *Zimmervermittlung*: a room-booking service at airports or major stations. *Fremdenverkehrsbüro* or *Fremdenverkehrsamt*: the tourist information office, which offers a similar service.

| Pension/Fremdenheim | guest house |
| Jugendherberge | youth hostel |

BOOKING A ROOM

Do you have an accommodation list?	Haben Sie ein Hotelverzeichnis? *haaben zee I-n hohtel-fair-tsyshniss?*
Can you reserve a room for me/us?	Können Sie mir/uns ein Zimmer reservieren? *kurnen zee meer/oons I-n tsimmer reserveeren?*
...in a hotel	...in einem Hotel *in I-nem hohtel*
...in a guest house	...in einer Pension *in I-ner penziohn*
...in the town centre	...in der Stadtmitte *in dair shtat-mitter*
...near the airport/station	...in der Nähe vom Flughafen/Bahnhof *in dair nai-er fom flooghafen/baanhohf*
...for 1/2 nights	...für eine Nacht/zwei Nächte *fewr I-ner nakht/tsvy neshter*
I'm not sure yet how long we'll stay	Ich weiß noch nicht, wie lange wir bleiben *ish vys nokh nisht, vee langer veer blyben*
Do you have anything cheaper/better?	Haben Sie etwas Billigeres/Besseres? *haaben zee etvas biligeres/besseres?*
How do I get there?	Wie komme ich dahin? *vee komer ish dahin?*

Can you show me on a street map?	Können Sie es mir auf einem Stadtplan zeigen? *kurnen zee es meer owf I-nem shtat-plan tsygen?*
What does it cost...?	Was kostet es...? *vas kostet es...?*
...per night	...pro Nacht *proh nakht*
...with breakfast	...mit Frühstück *mit frewstewk*
...with full/half board	...mit Vollpension/Halbpension *mit follpenziohn/halp-penziohn*
...for children	...für Kinder *fewr kinder*
Does that include breakfast/VAT?	Ist das mit Frühstück/ Mehrwertsteuer? *ist das mit frewstewk/ mairvairt-shtoyer?*
That's too expensive	Das ist mir zu teuer *das ist meer tsoo toyer*
I'd like a single room...	Ich möchte ein Einzelzimmer... *ish murshter I-n I-ntseltsimmer...*
We'd like a double room/ twin room...	Wir möchten ein Doppelzimmer/ Zweibettzimmer... *veer murshtun I-n doppel-tsimmer/ tsvy-bet-tsimmer...*
...with a bath	...mit Bad *mit baat*
...with a shower	...mit Dusche *mit doosher*
...with a balcony	...mit Balkon *mit balkohn*

Does it have cable/satellite TV?	Hat es Kabel-/ Satellitenfernsehen? *hat es kaabel/ zaturleeten-fairnsaihen?*
Do you have any vacancies?	Haben Sie ein Zimmer frei? *haaben zee I-n tsimmer fry?*
I/we have a reservation	Ich habe/wir haben ein Zimmer reserviert *ish haaber/veer haaben I-n tsimmer rezerveert*
My name is...	Ich heiße... *ish hyser...*
May I see the room?	Darf ich das Zimmer sehen? *daarf ish das tsimmer sai-en?*
It's too small/noisy	Es ist zu klein/laut *es ist tsoo klyn/lowt*
Can we have a child's cot?	Können wir ein Kinderbett haben? *kurnen veer I-n kinnderbet haaben?*
Could you have my luggage brought to my room?	Können Sie bitte mein Gepäck auf mein Zimmer bringen lassen? *kurnen zee bitter myn gerpek owf myn tsimmer bringen lassen?*
Where can I park my car?	Wo kann ich mein Auto parken? *voh kan ish myn owtoh parken?*
We'll take it	Wir nehmen es *veer naimen es*

You may see:

Rezeption	
Empfang	Reception
Anmeldung	
Abendessen	evening meal
Aufzug/Fahrstuhl	lift
belegt	no vacancies
Eingang	entrance
Erdgeschoss	ground floor
erster Stock	first floor
Frühstück	breakfast
Halbpension	half board
kein Zutritt	no entry
Mittagessen	lunch
nur für Gäste	patrons only
Rechnung	bill
Vollpension	full board
Zimmer frei	vacancies
Name	name
Vorname	forename
Nummer	number
Straße	road
Wohnort	town
Postleitzahl (Plz)	postcode
Geburtsdatum	date of birth
Geburtsort	place of birth
Passnummer	passport number
Datum	date
Unterschrift	signature

You will often be asked to fill in a registration form (*Anmeldeformular*).

You may hear:

Wir haben kein Zimmer
mehr frei
*veer haaben kyn tsimmer
mair fry*

We have no more rooms free

Wir sind voll belegt
veer sint foll berlaigt

We're full up

Wir haben keine
Doppelzimmer mehr frei
*veer haaben kyner
dopel-tsimmer mair fry*

We have no double rooms free

Wie heißen Sie?
vee hyssen zee?

What is your name?

Bitte füllen Sie das
Anmeldeformular aus
*bitter fewlen zee das
anmelder-formoolaar ows*

Please fill in the registration
form

Darf ich Ihren Pass sehen?
daarf ish eeren pass sai-en?

May I see your passport?

Unterschreiben Sie, bitte
oontershryben zee, bitter

Please sign this

Wie lange bleiben Sie?
vee langer blyben zee?

How long are you staying?

Ihre Zimmernummer ist...
eerer tsimmer-noomer ist...

Your room number is...

Das Zimmer ist im...
  ...Erdgeschoss
  ...ersten Stock
*das tsimmer ist im ...
  ...airdgeshoss
  ...airsten shtock*

The room is on the...
  ...ground floor
  ...first floor

Nehmen Sie den Aufzug
naimen zee dain owftsoog

Take the lift

ROOM SERVICE AND MEALS

What time is breakfast/ evening meal?	Wann gibt es Frühstück/ Abendessen? *van gipt ess frewstewk/ aabentessen?*
Can we have breakfast in our room?	Können wir auf unserem Zimmer frühstücken? *kurnen veer owf oonzerem tsimmer frewstewken?*
Please wake me at ... o'clock	Bitte wecken Sie mich um ... Uhr *bitter veken zee mish um ... oor*
May I have...?	Könnte ich ... haben? *kurnter ish ... haaben?*
...a bath towel	...ein Badetuch *I-n baadertookh*
...some clothes hangers	...einige Kleiderbügel *I-niger klyderbewgel*
...another pillow	...noch ein Kopfkissen *nokh I-n kopf-kissen*
...some soap	...Seife *zyfer*
...an ashtray	...einen Aschenbecher *I-nen ashen-bekher*
...an extra blanket	...eine extra Decke *I-ner extra dekker*
...a needle and thread	...eine Nadel und etwas Faden *I-ner naadel oont etvas faaden*
Can you get me a taxi?	Können Sie mir ein Taxi bestellen? *kurnen zee meer I-n taxi bershtellen?*

Can I phone direct from my room?	Kann ich von meinem Zimmer durchwählen? *kan ish von mynem tsimmer doorkh-vailen?*
Is there any post for me?	Ist Post für mich da? *ist posst fewr mish daa?*
My room number is...	Meine Zimmernummer ist... *myner tsimmer-noomer ist...*
What is my room number?	Welche Zimmernummer habe ich? *velscher tsimmer-noomer haaber ish?*
Could I have my key please?	Den Schlüssel, bitte *dain shlewssel bitter*
Can I leave this in the safe?	Kann ich das im Safe deponieren? *kan ish das im 'safe' deponeeren?*
I want these clothes cleaned/washed	Ich möchte diese Kleider reinigen/waschen lassen *ish murshter deezer klyder rynigern/vashern lassen*
I need them today/this evening/tomorrow	Ich brauche sie heute/heute Abend/Morgen *ish browkher zee hoyter/hoyter aabent/morgen*
Are there any messages for me?	Hat jemand eine Nachricht für mich hinterlassen? *hat Yaimant I-ner nakh-risht fewr mish hinterlassen?*
Is there room service?	Gibt es Zimmerservice? *gipt es tsimmer-surrvis?*

QUERIES AND COMPLAINTS

The...is broken/doesn't work/is blocked	...funktioniert nicht/ist kaputt/ist verstopft *foonktsion**ee**rt nisht/ist kap**oo**t/ist fairsht**o**pft*
...heating...	Die Heizung... *dee h**y**tsoong...*
...light...	Das Licht... *das lisht...*
...plug (electric)...	Der Stecker... *dair sht**e**ker...*
...shutter...	Der Fensterladen... *dair f**e**nster-laaden...*
...shower...	Die Dusche... *dee d**oo**sher...*
...socket...	Die Steckdose... *dee sht**e**kdohzer...*
...television...	Der Fernseher... *dair f**ai**rnzai-er...*
...wash-basin...	Das Waschbecken... *das v**a**shbeken...*
...bath...	Die Badewanne... *dee b**aa**dervanner...*
...toilet...	Die Toilette... *dee twal**e**tter...*
...air conditioning...	Die Klimaanlage... *dee kl**ee**ma-anlaager...*
...radio...	Das Radio... *das r**aa**dio...*
How does ... work?	Wie funktioniert...? *vee foonktsion**ee**rt...?*
The window is jammed	Das Fenster klemmt *das f**e**nster klemmt*

The tap is dripping	Der Wasserhahn tropft *dair vasserhaan tropft*
The bulb has blown	Die Birne ist kaputt *dee beerner ist kapoot*
My room has not been cleaned	Mein Zimmer wurde nicht gereinigt *myn tsimmer voorder nisht ger-ynikt*
Can you get it repaired?	Können Sie es reparieren lassen? *kurnen zee es repareeren lassen?*
There isn't any hot water	Es gibt kein warmes Wasser *es gipt kyn vaarmes vasser*
Where is the...?	Wo ist...? *voh ist...?*
...dining-room	...der Speisesaal...? *dair shpyzer-zaal...?*
...lift	...der Fahrstuhl *dair faar-shtool*
...toilet	...die Toilette *dee twaletter*
Do you have any...?	Haben Sie...? *haaben zee...?*
...writing paper	...Schreibpapier *shryp-papeer*
...envelopes	...Briefumschläge *breef-oomshlaiger*
...stamps	...Briefmarken *breefmaarken*
Can I make a phone call from here?	Kann ich von hier telefonieren? *kan ish fon heer telefohneeren?*

CHECKING OUT

May I have the bill?	Können Sie mir bitte die Rechnung geben?
	kurnen zee meer bitter dee reshnoong gaiben?
Can I pay by credit card?	Kann ich mit Kreditkarte bezahlen?
	kan ish mit kredeet-karter bertsaalen?
I'm/we're leaving...	Ich fahre/wir fahren...ab
	ish faarer/veer faaren...ap
...tomorrow	...morgen...
	morgen...
...today	...heute...
	hoyter...
Can we have our luggage brought down?	Können Sie unser Gepäck herunterbringen lassen?
	kurnen zee oonzer gerpek hairoonter-bringen lassen?
I must leave at once	Ich muss sofort abreisen
	ish moos zofort ap-ryzen
Is everything included?	Ist alles inbegriffen?
	ist alles inbergriffen?
I think you've made a mistake (in the bill)	Ich glaube, Sie haben sich verrechnet
	ish glowber zee haaben zish fair-rekhnet
Can you call a taxi?	Können Sie bitte ein Taxi rufen?
	kurnen zee bitter I-n taxi roofen?
Here's the forwarding address	Hier ist meine Nachsendeadresse
	heer ist myner nakh-zender-adresser
I'm in a hurry	Ich habe es eilig
	ish haaber es I-lig

YOUTH HOSTEL

• There are separate dormitories for men and women, and you are advised to take your own sleeping bag.

Where is the youth hostel?	Wo ist die Jugendherberge, bitte? *voh ist dee Yoogent-hairbairger, bitter?*
Do you have any beds free?	Haben Sie noch Plätze frei? *haaben zee nokh pletser fry?*
We'd like to stay 1/2 nights	Wir möchten eine Nacht/zwei Nächte bleiben *veer murshten I-ner nakht/tsvy neshter blyben*
There's...	Wir sind... *veer zint...*
...1/2 boys	...ein Junge/zwei Jungen *I-n Yoonger/tsvy Yoongen*
...1/2 girls	...ein/zwei Mädchen *I-n/tsvy maidshen*
...1/2 adults	...ein Erwachsener/zwei Erwachsene *I-n/tsvy airvakhsener*
...1/2 children	...ein Kind/zwei Kinder *I-n kint/tsvy kinder*
Here's my membership card	Hier ist mein Ausweis *heer ist myn owsvys*
We need bed linen	Wir brauchen Bettwäsche *veer browkhen betvesher*

We'd like supper and breakfast

Wir möchten Abendbrot
und Frühstück
*veer murshten aabentbroht
oont frewstewk*

Where is...?

Wo ist...?
voh ist...?

...our dormitory

...unser Schlafraum
oonzer shlaafrowm

...the kitchen

...die Küche
dee kewsher

...the shower

...die Dusche
dee doosher

...the toilet

...die Toilette
dee twaletter

...the washroom

...der Waschraum
dair vashrowm

You may hear:

Wir sind voll belegt
veer zint fol berlaigt

We're full up

Wie viele Personen?
veefeeler pairzohnen?

How many people?

Wie viele Nächte?
veefeeler neshter?

How many nights?

Wie lange wollen Sie bleiben?
vee langer vollen zee blyben?

How long do you want
to stay?

Ihren (Ihre) Ausweis(e) bitte
eeren(eerer) owsvyz(er), bitter

May I have your
passport(s) please?

Möchten Sie Bettwäsche leihen?
murshten zee bet-vesher lyen?

Do you want bed linen?

Welche Mahlzeiten wollen Sie?
velsher maaltsyten vollen zee?

Which meals do you
want?

It is illegal to camp without permission.

CAMPING AND CARAVANNING

• There are thousands of campsites in Germany, Austria and Switzerland. Some, in mountain areas, are open all year round. The tourist office can help you to find a suitable site.

We're looking for a campsite	Wir suchen einen Campingplatz *veer zookhen I-nen kemping-plats*
Can we camp here?	Können wir hier zelten? *kurnen veer heer tselten?*
Are there any other campsites nearby?	Gibt es noch andere Campingplätze in der Nähe? *gipt es nokh anderer kemping-pletser in dair nai-er?*
Do you have any vacancies for...?	Haben Sie Platz für...? *haaben zee plats fewr...?*
...a tent?	...ein Zelt *I-n tselt*
...a caravan	...einen Wohnwagen *I-nen vohnvaagen*
...a motor-home	...ein Wohnmobil *I-n vohn-mobeel*
How much does it cost for...?	Wie viel kostet es für...? *veefeel kostet es fewr...?*
...a night	...eine Nacht *I-ner nakht*
...a week	...eine Woche *I-ner vokher*
...one person	...eine Person *I-ner pairsohn*
...a car	...ein Auto *I-n owtoh*

Does that include everything?	Ist alles im Preis inbegriffen? *ist ales im prys inbergriffen?*
Is/are there…?	Gibt es…? *gipt es…?*
…cooking facilities	…Kochgelegenheiten *kokh-gerlaigenhyten*
…electricity	…Stromanschluss *shtrohm-anshloos*
…shop	…einen Laden *I-nen laaden*
…showers	…Duschen *dooshen*
…a swimming pool	…ein Schwimmbad *I-n shvimbaad*
…washing machines	…Waschmaschinen *vashmasheenen*
Where can I get butane gas?	Wo kann ich Butangas bekommen? *voh kan ish bootaangas berkommen?*
Are there discounts for children?	Gibt es Rabatt für Kinder? *gipt es rabat fewr kinnder?*
Do you have…?	Haben Sie…? *haaben zee…?*
…ice	…Eis *I-s*
…gas	…Butangas *bootaangas*
Does the campsite close at night?	Schließt der Campingplatz nachts? *shleest dair kemping-plats nakhts?*
We're leaving today/tomorrow	Wir fahren heute/morgen ab *veer faaren hoyter/mohrgen ab*

VILLAS & APARTMENTS

• Cleaning is always included in the price.

I'd like an apartment...	Ich möchte eine Ferienwohnung... *ish murshter I-ner fairien vohnoong...*
...with one bedroom	...mit einem Schlafzimmer *mit I-nem shlaaf-tsimmer*
...with two bedrooms	...mit zwei Schlafzimmern *mit tsvy shlaaf-tsimmern*
...for four people	...für vier Personen *fewr feer pairzohnen*
...for a week	...für eine Woche *fewr I-ner vokher*
...for a fortnight	...für zwei Wochen *fewr tsvy vokhen*
Which floor is it on?	In welchem Stock ist es? *in velshem shtok ist es?*
Is...included?	Ist...inbegriffen? *ist...inbergriffen*
...everything...	...alles... *all-es...*
...the gas...	...das Gas... *das gas...*
...the water...	...das Wasser... *das vasser...*
...the electricity...	...der Strom... *dair shtrohm...*
When...?	Wann...? *van...?*
...is it cleaned	...wird geputzt *veert gerpootst*

...is the rubbish collected	...kommt die Müllabfuhr *kommt dee mewl-apfoor*
Does it have...?	Gibt es...? *gipt es...?*
...heating	...Heizung *hytsoong*
...a fridge	...einen Kühlschrank *I-nen kewlshrank*
...bedclothes	...Bettzeug *bet-tsoyg*
...crockery	...Geschirr *gersheer*
...cutlery	...Besteck *bershtek*
...a washing machine	...eine Waschmaschine *I-ner vashmasheener*
Is it fully equipped?	Ist es voll ausgestattet? *ist es fol owsgershtattet?*
Is it electric or gas?	Ist es elektrisch oder Gas? *ist es elektrish ohder gas?*
I need...	Ich brauche... *ish browkher...*
...an electrician	...einen Elektriker *I-nen elektriker*
...a plumber	...einen Klempner *I-nen klempner*
...a heating engineer	...einen Heizungsfachmann *I-nen hytsoongz-fakhman*

TRAVEL

ROAD

• Germany has an excellent transport system; the major cities are connected to one another and to the UK and USA by air. The clean and punctual trains of DB (Deutsche Bundesbahn – German Federal Railways) are part of a fully integrated transport network linking cities, towns and villages.

• Speed limits: motorways   no speed limit for cars,
                                                   except in busy areas
            built-up areas 50 km/h (30 mph)
            other roads 100 km/h (60 mph)

•Motorways: *Autobahnen* in Germany do not charge tolls, but a toll (*die Maut/die Gebühr*) is payable on some mountain roads and tunnels in Austria, and in Switzerland you must display a special sticker (*die Vignette*), available in Britain from the AA or RAC.

• Right of way: traffic coming from the right has priority at junctions, unless it's entering from, for example, a service road, or there is a priority sign (a yellow diamond, or an arrow in a triangle).

How do I get to (+ place name)/ to (+ building, street)...?	Wie komme ich nach/zu...? *vee kommer ish nakh/ tsoo...?*
How far is it to (+ place name)/ to (+ building, road)...?	Wie weit ist es nach/zu...? *vee vyt ist es nakh/ tsoo...?*
How long does it take?	Wie lange dauert es? *vee langer dowert es?*
Am I on the right road for...?	Bin ich auf der richtigen Straße nach...? *bin ish owf dair rishtigen shtraaser nakh...?*
Can you show it to me on the map/on the street map?	Können Sie es mir auf der Karte/auf dem Stadtplan zeigen? *kurnen zee es meer owf dair kaarter/ owf dem shtatplaan tsygen?*
Where can I park?	Wo kann ich parken? *vo kan ish parken?*

You may hear:

Nehmen Sie die Straße nach/über... *naimen zee dee shtraaser nakh/ewber...*	Take the road for/via...
Fahren Sie Richtung... *faaren zee rishtoong...*	Go in the direction of...

You should obtain a green card from your insurance company before taking your car abroad. Additional breakdown policies are also available. For full details contact the AA or RAC.

Sie sind auf der falschen Straße
zee zint owf dair falshen shtraaser

You're on the wrong road

Sie müssen zurück nach...
zee mewssen tsoorewk nakh...

You'll have to go back to...

nördlich/südlich von...
nurdlish/sewdlish fon...

to the north/south of...

östlich/westlich von...
urstlish/vestlish fon...

to the east/west of...

Fahren Sie...
faaren zee...

Go...

...geradeaus
geraaderows

...straight on

...nach links
nakh links

...left

...nach rechts
nakh reshts

...right

...bis zur ersten/zweiten
Kreuzung
*bis tsoor airsten/ tsvyten
kroytsoong*

...to the first/ second
junction

...bis zur Ampel
bis tsoor ampel

...to the traffic lights

FILLING STATION/GARAGE

Where's the nearest filling
station/garage?

Wo ist die nächste
Tankstelle/
Reparaturwerkstatt?
*vo ist dee neshste tank-
shteller/reparatoor-vairk-shtat?*

Please fill the tank

Volltanken, bitte
foltanken, bitter

lead-free

bleifrei/unverbleit
blyfry/oonfairblyt

diesel	Diesel *deezel*
Please check/change/repair	Bitte überprüfen/wechseln/ reparieren Sie … *bitter ewbrprewfen/veshseln/ repareeren zee …*
…the oil	…das Öl *das url*
…the water	…das Kühlwasser *das kewlvasser*
…the brake fluid	…die Bremsflüssigkeit *dee brems-flewsigkyt*
…the tyre	…den Reifen *dain ryfen*
…the spare tyre	…den Ersatzreifen *dain erzats-ryfen*
…the battery	…die Batterie *dee bateree*
…the bulb	…die Glühbirne *dee glew-beerner*
…the fanbelt	…den Keilriemen *dain kylreemen*
…the fuse	…die Sicherung *dee zisheroong*
…the spark plugs	…die Zündkerzen *dee tsewnt-kairtsen*
…the windscreen	…die Windschutzscheibe *dee vintshoots-shyber*
…the brakes	…die Bremsen *dee bremzen*
…the exhaust pipe	…den Auspuff *dain owspoof*

...the radiator	...den Kühler *dain kewler*
Can you help me?	Können Sie mir helfen? *kurnun zee meer helfen?*
Do you do repairs?	Machen sie Reparaturen? *makhen zee reparatooren?*
The engine's running hot	Der Motor läuft heiß *dair motohr loyft hyss*

BREAKDOWN

Where's the nearest garage?	Wo ist die nächste Reparaturwerkstatt? *voh ist dee neshster reparatoor-vairk-shtat?*
I've had a breakdown	Ich habe eine Panne *ish haaber I-ner panner*
I've got a flat tyre	Ich habe einen Platten *ish haaber I-nen platten*
I've run out of petrol	Mir ist das Benzin ausgegangen *meer ist das bentseen owsgergangen*
The engine won't start	Der Motor springt nicht an *dair motohr shpringt nisht an*
The engine is overheating	Der Motor läuft heiß *dair motohr loyft hyss*
The battery is flat	Die Batterie ist leer *dee bateree ist lair*
There's something wrong with the...	...ist nicht in Ordnung *ist nisht in ordnoong*
Please send a mechanic/ a breakdown truck	Bitte schicken Sie einen Mechaniker/einen Abschleppwagen *bitter shikken zee I-nen mekaaniker/ I-nen abshlep-vaagen*

I'm on the road from...to...	Ich bin auf der Straße zwischen...und...
	ish bin owf dair shtraasser tsvishen...oont...
I'm 5 kilometers from...	Ich bin fünf Kilometer von...
	ish bin fewnf kilomaiter fon...
How long will it take?	Wie lange dauert es?
	vee langer dowert es?

See page 156 for numbers.

ROAD TRAVEL

You may see:

Anliegerverkehr frei/ Nur für Anlieger	access to residents/ owners only
Ausfahrt	exit
Bahnübergang	railway crossing
Baustelle	roadworks
Durchgangsverkehr	through traffic
Einbahnstraße	one-way street
Einordnen	get in lane
Fahrradweg	cycle path
Fußgängerzone	pedestrian zone
Gefährliche Kurve	dangerous bend
Gegenverkehr	two-way traffic
Gesperrt für Fahrzeuge	closed to vehicles
Glatteis	black ice
Halteverbot	no stopping
Kriechspur	slow lane/crawler lane
Langsam fahren	slow

Most roadsigns are identical to those found in Britain. The words and phrases listed on this page are commonly found on roadsigns and notices.

Lkw	lorry/truck
Nicht überholen	no overtaking
Nur für Busse/Pkw	Buses/cars only
Parken nur mit Parkscheibe	Parking disc holders only
Parkplatz	car-park
Parkscheibe/Parkuhren	parking disc/parking meters
Pkw	car
Raststätte	services
Überholen verboten	no overtaking
Umleitung	diversion
...verboten	no...
Vorsicht	caution

BUYING TICKETS

When is the next train to Bonn?	Wann fährt der nächste Zug nach Bonn?
	van fairt dair neshster tsoog nakh bon?
When does it arrive?	Wann kommt er an?
	van komt air an?
Do I have to change?	Muss ich umsteigen?
	moos ish oomshtygen?
I'd like a ... ticket to Bonn	Ich möchte eine Fahrkarte nach Bonn...
	ish murshter I-ner faarkaarter nakh bon...
...single (one way)	...einfach
	I-nfakh
...return	...hin und zurück
	hin oont zoorewk
...first class	...erster Klasse
	airster klasser

...second class	...zweiter Klasse *tsvyter klasser*
What does it cost?	Was kostet es? *vos kostet es?*
What about children?	Und für Kinder? *oont fewr kinnder?*
Are there reductions for children/students?	Gibt es Ermäßigungen für Kinder/Studenten? *gipt es airmaissigoongen fewr kinnder/shtoodenten?*
I'm a (non-)smoker	Ich bin (Nicht-)Raucher *ish bin (nisht-)rowkher*

BUYING TICKETS – AIR

Is it a direct flight?	Ist es ein Direktflug? *ist es I-n direktfloog?*
Is there a connection to Munich?	Gibt es einen Anschluss nach München? *gipt es I-nen an-shloos nakh mewnchen?*
When does the plane take off?	Wann ist der Abflug? *van ist dair abfloog?*
When do we land?	Wann landen wir? *van landen veer?*
What is the flight number?	Welche Flugnummer ist es? *velsher floog-noomer ist es?*
When must I check in?	Wann muss ich einchecken? *van moos ish I-ncheken?*
Is there an airport bus?	Gibt es einen Flughafenbus? *gipt es I-nen flooghaafen-boos?*
I'd like to...my reservation	Ich möchte meine Reservierung... *ish murshter myner rezerveeroong...*

...confirm	...bestätigen *bershtaitigen*
...alter	...umbuchen *oombooken*
...cancel	...annullieren *anulleeren*

You may see:

Abfahrt	Departures
Ankunft	Arrivals
Fluggäste/Passagiere	Passengers
Fluglinie	Airline
Gepäckausgabe	Luggage reclaim
Inland	Internal (flights)
Linienflug	Scheduled flight
Passkontrolle	Passport control
Zoll	Customs
Zollfreie Waren	Duty-free shop

RAIL

• The main types of train are:

TEE-Zug: Trans European Express (1st class only – supplement [*Zuschlag*] payable)

ICE: Inter City Express – first class supplement [*Zuschlag*] payable.

D-Zug: Express (supplement payable for journeys under 50km) (*Städteschnellzug* in Austria, *Schnellzug* in Austria, Switzerland)

E-Zug: Moderately fast train - does not stop at small stations.

N-Zug: Local train stopping at all stations (*Personenzug* in Austria, *Regionalzug* in Switzerland)

• Coaches on long-distance international trains are often regrouped along their route for different destinations. It is important to get on the right *Kurswagen* by checking the destination plate on the coaches; you can find the approximate position of the coach beforehand by looking at the *Wagenstandanzeiger* on the platform.

- Remember that German railways show two timetables:

    Abfahrt Departures   *Ankunft* Arrivals

- Other useful terms are:

    Speisewagen Dining car

    Schlafwagen Sleeping car with compartments containing a washbasin and one, two or three berths.

    Liegewagen Coach containing berths with sheets, blankets and pillows. Cheaper than the Schlafwagen.

- It is advisable to reserve your seat or berth in advance.

- German railway stations have luggage lockers where luggage may be left.

AT THE STATION

Where is/are the...?	Wo ist/sind...?
	voh ist/zind...?
...(currency) exchange office	...die Wechselstube
	dee <u>vesh</u>sel-shtoober
...left-luggage counter (baggage check)	...die Gepäck- aufbewahrung
	dee ger<u>peck</u>- owfbervaaroong
...lost property office	...das Fundbüro
	das <u>foont</u>-bewroh
...luggage check-in	...die Gepäckaufgabe
	dee ger<u>peck</u>-owfgaaber
...luggage check-out	...die Gepäckausgabe
	dee ger<u>peck</u>-owsgaaber

If you do not have time to buy a ticket before boarding the train, you may buy one from the guard (*Schaffner*) on the train, as long as you go and find him as soon as possible.

...news-stand	...das Zeitungskiosk
	das tystoongs-kee-osk
...platform 2	...Gleis 2/Bahnsteig 2
	glys tsvy/baan-shtyg tsvy
...reservations office	...die Platzreservierung
	dee plats-reserveeroong
...restaurant	...das Restaurant
	das restaurong
...snack bar	...der Schnellimbiss
	dair shnel-imbis
...ticket office/counter	...der Fahrkartenschalter
	dair faar-kaarten-shalter
...waiting room	...der Wartesaal
	dair vaarter-zaal
...the toilets	...die Toiletten
	dee twaletten
...luggage-lockers	...die Schließfächer
	dee shlees-fesher
...luggage-trolleys	...die Kofferkulis
	dee koffer-kooliz
I'd like to reserve...	Ich möchte...reservieren
	ish murshter...rezerveeren
...a seat/2 seats	...einen Platz/zwei Plätze
	I-nen plats/tsvy pletser
...by the window	...am Fenster
	am fenster
...in a no-smoking compartment	...in einem Nichtraucherabteil
	in I-nem nisht-rowkherabtyl
...in a smoking compartment	...in einem Raucherabteil
	in I-nem rowkherabytl
...a berth in a sleeping car	...einen Platz im Schlafwagen
	I-nen plats in shlaafvaagen

Do I have to pay a surcharge?	Muss ich einen Zuschlag bezahlen? *moos ish I-nen tsoo-shlaag bertsaalen?*
Will the train leave on time?	Fährt der Zug pünktlich ab? *fairt dair tsoog pewnktlish ap?*
Will the train arrive on time?	Kommt der Zug pünktlich an? *komt dair tsoog pewnktlish an?*
Is there enough time to change?	Reicht die Zeit zum Umsteigen? *rysht dee tsyt tsoom oomshtygen?*
Does the train stop in Bonn?	Hält der Zug in Bonn? *helt dair tsoog in bonn?*
What platform does the train to Bonn leave from?	Auf welchem Gleis fährt der Zug nach Bonn ab? *owf velshem glys fairt dair tsoog nakh bonn ap?*
Does the train have a restaurant car/ sleeping car?	Führt der Zug einen Speisewagen/einen Schlafwagen? *fewrt dair tsoog I-nen shpyzer-vaagen/I-nen shlaaf-vaagen?*
Is this the train to Bonn?	Ist das der Zug nach Bonn? *ist das dair tsoog nakh bonn?*
I'd like to register (check) my luggage	Ich möchte mein Gepäck aufgeben *ish murshter myn gerpeck owfgaiben*

ON THE TRAIN

Is this seat free?	Ist dieser Platz frei? *ist deezer plats fry?*
This seat's taken	Dieser Platz ist besetzt *deezer plats ist berzetst*

I think this is my seat	Ich glaube, das ist mein Platz
	ish glowber, das ist myn plats
I have a reservation for this seat	Ich habe eine Reservierung für diesen Platz
	ish haaber I-ner resairveeroong fewr deezen plats.
Excuse me. May I come past?	Entschuldigung. Kann ich bitte durch?
	ent-shooldigoong, kan ish bitter doorsh?
What's this place called?	Wie heißt dieser Ort?
	vee hyst deezer ort?
How long will the train stop here?	Wie lange hält der Zug hier?
	vee langer helt dair tsoog heer?
Where is my berth?	Wo ist meine Kabine?
	voh ist myner kabeener?
Please wake me at 6	Bitte wecken Sie mich um 6 Uhr
	bitter veken zee mish um zekhs oor
Would you bring me coffee at 6?	Würden Sie mir bitte um 6 Uhr Kaffee bringen?
	vewrden zee meer bitter oom zekhs oor kafai bringen?
Can you tell me when we get to…?	Sagen Sie mir bitte Bescheid, wenn wir in…ankommen…?
	zaagen zee meer bitter bershyt ven veer in…ankommen…?
Where are we?	Wo sind wir hier?
	voh zint veer heer?

You may hear:

| Der nächste Zug nach Bonn fährt um… | The next train to Bonn leaves at… |
| *dair neshster tsoog nakh bonn fairt oom…* | |

Steigen Sie in…um *shtygen zee in…oom*	Change in…
Sie müssen einen Zuschlag bezahlen *zee mewssen I-nen tsooshlaag bertsaalen*	You must pay a supplement
Der Fahrkartenschalter ist… *dair faarkartenshalter ist…*	The ticket office is…
…da drüben *da drewben*	…over there
…links *links*	…on the left
…rechts *reshts*	…on the right
…oben *ohben*	…upstairs
…unten *oonten*	…downstairs
Der Zug hat…Minuten Verspätung *dair tsoog hat…minooten fairshpaitoong*	The train will be…minutes late
Erste Klasse…des Zuges *airster klaser…des tsooges*	First class…of the train
…an der Spitze… *an dair shpitser…*	…at the front…
…in der Mitte… *in dair mitter…*	…in the middle…
…am Ende… *am ender…*	…at the end…

You may see or hear:
(See also pages 64–66)

Achtung/Vorsicht! *akhtoong/fohrzisht*	Attention/watch out!
aussteigen *ows-shtygen*	to get off/out
einsteigen *I-nshtygen*	to get in/on
Nichtraucher *nisht-rowkher*	non-smoker
Notbremse *nohtbremzer*	emergency cord
planmäßig *plaan-maisig*	scheduled
Platzkarte *plats-kaarter*	seat reservation
Raucher *rowkher*	smoker
sonn- und feiertags *zon oont fyertaagz*	Sundays and holidays
Strecke *shtreker*	route
umsteigen *oomshtygen*	to change
verkehrt nicht an... *fairkairt nisht an...*	does not run on...(days)
verkehrt nur an... *fairkairt noor an...*	runs only on...(days)
Zug fährt sofort ab! *tsoog fairt zofort ab!*	train now leaving!
zurücktreten! *tsoorewk-traiten!*	stand clear!

zuschlagpflichtig
tsooshlag-pflishtig

subject to supplementary fare
(see note on page 52)

BUS, TRAM AND UNDERGROUND

• Local transport consists of buses, and in the larger cities, trams, underground and the S-bahn (local rail/underground network).

• Tickets, which may be used on any form of local transport, vary in cost according to the number of zones crossed. Ticket machines usually give change.

• In rural areas, rail links tie in with the bus services run by DB (red) or the Post Office (yellow).

• Automatic ticket dispensers (*Fahrkartenautomat*) are widespread. If you intend to make a number of journeys it may be worth your while to buy a booklet of tickets.

I'd like a book of tickets	Ich möchte eine Sammelkarte *ish murshter I-ner zammel-kaarter*
Where is the...?	Wo ist...? *voh ist...?*
...bus stop	...die Haltestelle *dee halter-shtelle*
...bus station	...der Busbahnhof *dair boosbaanhohf*
...underground station	...die U-Bahn-Station *dee oobaarn-statsyohn*
Does this bus stop in...?	Hält dieser Bus in...? *helt deezer boos in...?*
Can you tell me where to	Können Sie mir bitte

Tickets must usually be passed through an automatic stamping machine (*Entwerter*) as you get on the bus, tram or underground (subway).

get off, please?	Bescheid sagen, wo ich aussteigen muss? *kurnen zee meer bitter bershyt zaagen, voh ish ows-shtygen moos?*
I'd like to get off here	Ich möchte hier aussteigen *ish murshter ows-shtygen*
Does this bus go to...?	Fährt dieser Bus...? *fairt deezer boos...?*
Which bus goes to...?	Welcher Bus fährt...? *velsher boos fairt...?*
How often are the buses to...?	Wie oft fahren die Busse...? *vie oft faaren dee booser...?*
How many stops to...?	Wie viele Haltestellen sind es bis...? *veefeeler halter-shtellen zint es bis...?*
...the cathedral	...zum Dom *tsoom dohm*
...the museum	...zum Museum *tsoom moozai-oom*
...the Old Town	...zur Altstadt *tsoor alt-shtat*
...the theatre	...zum Theater *tsoom tai-aater*
...the youth hostel	...zur Jugendherberge *tsoor Yoogent-hairbairger*
...Würzburg	...nach Würzburg *nakh vewrtsboorg*
When is the next bus to...?	Wann fährt der nächste Bus nach...? *van fairt dair neshster boos nakh...?*

| How much is the fare to...? | Was kostet es nach...? |
| | *vas kostet es nakh...?* |

You may hear:

| Nehmen Sie Bus Linie 6 | Take a number 6 |
| *naimen zee boos leenyer zekhs* | |

| Ein Bus fährt alle 10 Minuten | A bus leaves every 10 minutes |
| *I-n boos fairt aller tsain minooten* | |

You may see:

| Bushaltestelle | regular bus stop |
| Bedarfshaltestelle | stops on request |

BOATS AND FERRIES

| When is there a boat for...? | Wann fährt ein Schiff nach...? |
| | *van fairt I-n shif nakh...?* |

| Where does it leave from? | Wo fährt es ab? |
| | *voh fairt es ap?* |

| When do we call in...? | Wann legen wir in...an? |
| | *van laigen veer in...an?* |

| How long does the crossing last? | Wie lange dauert die Überfahrt? |
| | *vee langer dowert dee ewberfaart?* |

| We'd like a trip on the river | Wir möchten eine Flussfahrt machen |
| | *veer murshten I-ner floos-faart makhen* |

| We'd like a cabin | Wir möchten eine Kabine |
| | *veer murshten I-ner kubeener* |

| There's... | Wir sind... |
| | *veer zint...* |

| ...1 adult/2 adults | ...ein Erwachsener/zwei Erwachsene |
| | *I-n airvakhsener/tsvy airvakhsener* |

Look for the sign *Taxistand* (taxi rank). It is not usual to hail a taxi.
Tipping: about 10%.

...1 child/2 chidren	...ein Kind/zwei Kinder *I-n kint/tsvy kinnder*
We have...	Wir haben... *veer haaben...*
...a car	...ein Auto *I-n owtoh*
...bicycles	...Fahrräder *faar-raider*
...a caravan	...einen Wohnwagen *I-nen vohn-vaagen*
...a motorbike	...ein Motorrad *I-n motohr-raat*

TAXI

Where can I get a taxi?	Wo finde ich ein Taxi? *voh finder ish I-n taxi?*
Please get me a taxi	Können Sie mir bitte ein Taxi rufen? *kurnen zee meer bitter I-n taxi roofen?*
Please take me to...	Fahren Sie mich bitte... *faaren zee mish bitter...*
...this address	...zu dieser Adresse *tsoo deezer addresser*
...the station	...zum Bahnhof *tsoom baanhof*
...the airport	...zum Flughafen *tsoom flooghaafen*
Could you help me with my luggage?	Können Sie mir mit meinem Gepäck helfen? *kurnen zee meer mit mynem gerpeck helfen?*
Please stop here	Bitte halten Sie hier *bitter halten zee heer*

Wait for me, please	Bitte warten Sie auf mich *bitter vaarten zee owf mish*
How much is it?	Was kostet es? *vas kostet es?*
Keep the change	Es stimmt so *es shtimmt zoh*
Can you give me a receipt?	Können Sie mir bitte eine Quittung geben? *kurnen zee meer bitter I-ner kvitoong gaiben?*

CAR HIRE

I'd like to hire a car	Ich möchte ein Auto mieten *ish murshter I-n owtoh meeten*
I'd like a small/medium/ large one	Ich möchte ein kleines/ eine mittelgroßes/ ein großes *ish murshter I-n klynes/ I-n mittelgrohses/ I-n grohses*
I'd like it for...	Ich möchte es für... *ish murshter es fewr...*
...a day	...einen Tag *I-nen taag*
...2 days	...zwei Tage *tsvy taager*
...a week	...eine Woche *I-ner vokher*
What are the tariffs per day/week?	Was sind die Tarife pro Tag/pro Woche? *vas zint dee tareefer proh taag/proh vokher?*

Look for the sign *Autoverleih* or *Autovermietung*.

Can I leave the car in...?	Kann ich das Auto in ... zurück-geben? *kan ish das owtoh in ... tsoorewk-gaiben?*
I'd like comprehensive insurance	Ich möchte eine Vollkaskoversicherung *ish murshter I-ner folkaskoh-fairzisheroong*
How much deposit must I pay?	Wie viel muss ich hinterlegen? *veefeel moos ish hinterlaigen?*
Here is my driving licence/ my passport	Hier ist mein Führerschein/ mein Pass *heer ist myn fewrershyn/myn pass*

You may see:

Abfahrt	Departures
Abflug	Departures (airport)
Ankunft	Arrivals
Ausgang	Exit
Auskunft	Information
Ausland	abroad
Bahnhofspolizei	railway police
Behinderte	disabled
besetzt	occupied
bezahlen	pay
Damen	ladies
Eingang	Entrance
Einstieg nur mit Fahrausweis	buy ticket before boarding
Einstieg vorn/hinten	board at front/rear
einwerfen	insert
entwerten	stamp, validate (ticket)

Erwachsene	adult
Fahrausweis/Fahrkarte/Fahrschein	ticket
Fahrgäste	passengers
Fahrplan	timetable
Familienkarte	family ticket
Flughafenbus	airport bus
Flugplan	flight schedule
Flugsteig	gate
frei	free
Geldeinwurf	insert money here
Geldrückgabe	returned coins
Gepäckschließfächer	luggage lockers
Gleis	platform
Gruppenkarte	group ticket
Hafen	port, harbour
Haltestelle	bus/tram stop
Hauptbahnhof (Hbf)	main station
Herren	men
Imbiss	snack (-bar)
Inland	domestic
kein Ausstieg/Einstieg	no exit/entry
kein Zugang	no entry
Kinder	children
Kurswagen	through coach
Mehrfahrtenkarte	multi-journey ticket
Minigruppenkarte	group ticket (4 people)
Monatskarte	monthly card
Münzen	coins

Netz	**network**
Nichtraucher	**non-smoker (compartment)**
nicht hinauslehnen	**do not lean out**
Notausgang	**emergency exit**
nur werktags	**weekdays only**
Raucher	**smoker (compartment)**
Reiseauskunft	**travel information**
samstags	**Saturdays**
S-Bahn	**local railway network**
Senioren	**senior citizens**
sonn -und feiertags	**Sundays and public holidays**
Strecke	**route**
Tageskarte	**day ticket**
U-Bahn	**tube, underground**
Wagenstandanzeiger	**Order of carriages** (see introductory note on page 53)
Wartesaal	**waiting room**
zu den Gleisen/Zügen	**to the platforms/trains**
zuschlagflichtig	**supplement payable**

SIGHTSEEING

Where's the information office?	Wo ist das Informationsbüro? *voh ist das informatsyohns-bewroh?*
What are the main places of interest?	Was sind die Hauptsehens-würdigkeiten? *vas zint dee howpt-zaiens-vewrdikh-kyten?*
What is there of interest to children?	Was ist für Kinder interessant? *vas ist fewr kinnder interessant?*

Do you have a street map?	Haben sie einen Stadtplan? *haabun zee I-nen* *shtat-plaan?*
Is it easy to get there on foot?	Kann man das leicht zu Fuss erreichen? *kan man das lysht tsoo* *fooss airyshen?*
Where is/are the...?	Wo ist/sind...? *voh ist/zint...?*
...art gallery	...die Kunstgalerie *dee koonstgalleree*
...castle	...das Schloss/die Burg *das shlos/dee boorg*
...cathedral	...die Kathedrale/der Dom *dee katedraaler/dair* *dohm*
...church	...die Kirche *dee keersher*
...concert hall	...die Konzerthalle *dee kontsairt-haller*
...conference centre	...die Kongresshalle *dee kongress-haller*
...exhibition centre	...das Messegelände *das messer-gerlender*
...market place	...der Marktplatz *dair maarkt-plats*
...museum	...das Museum *das moozai-um*
...shopping centre	...das Einkaufszentrum *das I-nkowfs-tsentroom*
...sports centre	...das Sportzentrum *das shport-tsentroom*

Most towns have a tourist information office, signposted with a large letter 'i'. They can help with information not only about places of interest and events, but also booking accommodation.

...town centre	...die Innenstadt *dee innen-shtat*
Is the...worth visiting?	Ist...sehenswert? *ist...zai-enzvairt?*
Have we got time to visit...?	Haben wir noch Zeit, ...zu besichtigen? *haaben veer nokh tsyt, ...tsoo berzishtigen?*
I'm interested in...	Ich interessiere mich für... *ish interesseerer mish fewr...*
...archaeology	...Archäologie *arsh-eh-ologee*
...art	...Kunst *koonst*
...history	...Geschichte *ger-shishter*
...music	...Musik *moozeek*
...natural history	...Naturkunde *natoor-koonder*
...technology	...Technik *teshnik*

ADMISSION

Is it open on Saturdays/today/tomorrow?	Ist es samstags/heute/morgen geöffnet? *ist es zamztaagz/hoyter/morgen ger-urfnet?*
What are the opening times?	Was sind die Öffnungszeiten? *vas zint dee urfnoongz-tsyten?*
There are four of us	Wir sind 4 Personen *veer zint feer pairzohnen*

2 adults/children	2 Erwachsene/Kinder *tsvy airvakhsener/kinnder*
I'd like a guide book (in English)	Ich möchte einen Reiseführer (auf Englisch) *ish murshter I-nen ryzer-fewrer (owf ennglish)*
When does it close?	Wann schließt es? *van shleest es?*
How much does it cost to go in?	Was kostest der Eintritt? *vas kostest dair I-ntritt?*
Is it suitable for disabled people?	Ist es behindertengerecht? *ist es berhinderten-geresht?*
Is there wheelchair access?	Kann man mit einem Rollstuhl hinein? *kan man mit I-nen rol-shtool hin-In?*
Can I take photographs?	Darf man fotografieren? *darf man fohtografeeren?*
Are there special rates for...?	Gibt es Ermäßigungen für...? *gipt es air-maissigoongen fewr...?*
...children	...Kinder *kinnder*
...disabled people	...Behinderte *ber-hinnderter*
...groups	...Gruppen *groopen*
...pensioners/senior citizens	...Rentner/Senioren *rentner/zeniohren*
....students	...Studenten *shtoodenten*

In the mountain areas, signposts show distances in hours rather than kilometres.

You may see:

Eintrittspreise	Admission charges
Eintritt frei	Admission free
Fotografieren verboten	} No photography
Fotografieren nicht gestattet	
Rauchen verboten	No smoking

IN THE COUNTRY

• The countryside and forests are crisscrossed with large numbers of well-marked footpaths (*Wanderwege*). A map showing the footpaths in the locality (*eine Wanderkarte*) will help you get the best out of these.

How far is it to...?	Wie weit ist es nach...? *vee vyt ist es nakh...?*
How long will it take?	Wie lange dauert es? *vee langer dowert es?*
How do I get to...?	Wie komme ich nach...? *vee kommer ish nakh...?*
Is there a pub near here?	Ist ein Gasthaus in der Nähe? *ist I-n gast-hous in dair naier?*
Where does this footpath/ road lead to?	Wohin führt dieser Fußweg/diese Straße? *voh-hin fewrt deezer fooss-vaig/deezer shtraasser?*
What's the name of this...?	Wie heißt...? *vee hysst...?*
...castle	...das Schloss *das shloss*
...lake	...der See *dair zai*

...river	...der Fluss *dair flooss*
...village	...das Dorf *das dorf*
What's that called in German?	Wie heißt das auf Deutsch? *vee hysst das owf doych?*

DESCRIBING THINGS AND PLACES

It's...	Es ist... *es ist...*
...amazing	...erstaunlich *air-sht<u>ow</u>nlish*
...awful	...schrecklich *shr<u>e</u>klish*
...beautiful	...schön *shurn*
...boring	...langweilig *l<u>a</u>ngvylig*
...depressing	...deprimierend *deprim<u>ee</u>rent*
...impressive	...beeindruckend *ber-<u>I</u>-ndrookent*
...interesting	...interessant *interess<u>a</u>nt*
...lovely	...wunderschön *v<u>oo</u>ndershurn*
...picturesque	...malerisch *m<u>aa</u>lerish*
...pretty	...hübsch *hewpsh*
...romantic	...romantisch *rohm<u>a</u>ntish*

...strange	...seltsam *zeltzaam*
...ugly	...hässlich *hesslish*
I (don't) like it	Es gefällt mir (nicht) *es gerfelt meer (nisht)*

EATING OUT

• There is a special **What's on the menu?** section listing items of food and German specialities on page 88.

• It is possible to buy a meal at any time of day, and well into the evening, in Germany, Austria and Switzerland. You will find foreign restaurants (particularly Italian) and fast-food cafeterias as well as the usual cafés and pubs where you can eat *gut bürgerlich* (good home-cooking).

• Each area has its own specialities of dishes, breads, cakes, sausages, and beers or wines.

In all but fast-food shops and snack- bars, there will be waiters or waitresses. German law allows children and young people to buy alcohol (but not spirits) at 14 if accompanied by an adult, 16 if not. Children are allowed in pubs.

PLACES TO EAT AND DRINK

Brauhaus/ Bierstube Rather like a pub or tavern. The emphasis is on beer rather than food.

Café/ Café-Konditorei Coffee shop. The cheapest are self-service cafés where the customers stand at small high tables. Cafés are often linked to a *Konditorei*, a cake/pastry shop. If you want a slice of cake with your drink, make your selection out in the shop (unless you know the name of what you want); you will be given a piece of paper (*ein Zettel*) which you give to the waitress when you place your drinks order.

Gasthaus/ Gasthof Inn; found in the country or in small towns, with snacks, full meals and drinks on offer.

Gaststätte Restaurant.

Kaffeehaus Café, in Austria.

Raststätte/ Rasthof Motorway services and restaurant.

Ratskeller/ Ratstube Café or restaurant near to, or in the cellar of, the town hall.

Schnellimbiss/ Imbiss Snack bar, selling mainly beer and sausages.

Weinstube Rather like a Gasthof; found in wine-producing areas.

You may see:

Heute Ruhetag	Closed today
Montag Betriebsruhe	Closed on Mondays
Durchgehend warme Küche	Hot meals available all day
Straßenverkauf Zum Mitnehmen }	Take away
Reserviert	Reserved
Stammtisch	Table reserved for landlord and regulars (in pubs)

Meals

Breakfast *(das Frühstück)*: a fairly substantial meal of bread, rolls, cheese, cold meats and sausages, and jam, accompanied by coffee, tea, milk, and/ or fruit juice.

Lunch *(das Mittagessen)*: this is often the main meal of the day, and is usually accompanied by salads. It is often not followed by a pudding.

Evening meal *(das Abendessen)*: when taken at home, it is often rather like breakfast; when guests are invited, or in restaurants, a cooked meal is more normal.

Afternoon tea *(Kaffee und Kuchen)*: this is often taken at weekends, and usually consists of coffee and various cakes/ pastries.

RESERVATIONS

Have you got a table free?	Haben Sie einen Tisch frei? *haaben zee I-nen tish fry?*
I'd like to reserve a table for 4	Ich möchte einen Tisch für vier reservieren *ish murshter I-nen tish fewr feer rezerveeren*
We're coming at 9	Wir kommen um neun *veer kommen oom noyn*
We'd like a table...	Wir möchten einen Tisch... *veer murshten I-nen tish...*
...by the window	...am Fenster *am fenster*
...in a no-smoking area	...in der Nichtraucherecke *in dair nisht-rowkher-eker*
...outside	...im Freien *im fryen*

Don't sit at a table marked *Stammtisch* – it's reserved for a particular group of regular customers.

...on the terrace	...auf der Terrasse *owf dair tairasser*
My name is...	Ich heiße... *ish hysser...*
Can I pay by credit card?	Kann ich mit Kreditkarte bezahlen? *kan ish mit kredeetkarter bertsaalen?*
I have a reservation	Ich habe reserviert *ish haaber resairveert*

ORDERING

Waiter/ Waitress	Herr Ober/Bedienung! *hair ohber/berdeenoong!*
May I have the menu, please?	Kann ich die Speisekarte haben, bitte? *kan ish dee shpyzer-kaarter haaben, bitter?*
May we have the wine list, please?	Können wir die Weinkarte haben, bitte? *kurnen veer dee vynkaarter haaben, bitter?*
I'm/ We're ready to order now	Ich möchte/Wir möchten jetzt bestellen *ish murshter/veer murshten yetst bershtellen*
I/ We haven't decided yet	Ich bin/Wir sind noch nicht so weit *ish bin/veer zint nokh nisht zoh vyt*
I/ We'll order something to drink first	Ich bestelle/Wir bestellen zuerst etwas zu trinken *ish bershtelle/veer bershtellen tsooairst etvas tsoo trinken*

When ordering a meal in an inn it is worth bearing in mind that the main courses are substantial; a starter and a pudding are often unnecessary, unless you're very hungry.

Do you have any...?	Haben Sie...?
	haaben zee...?
I'd just like a snack	Ich möchte nur eine Kleinigkeit essen
	ish murshter noor I-ner klynigkyt essen
What do you recommend?	Was empfehlen Sie?
	vas empfailen zee?
Do you have any local dishes?	Haben Sie Gerichte aus der Gegend?
	haaben zee gerishter ows dair gaigent?
What is that?	Was ist das?
	vas ist das?
Is salad/ vegetables included?	Ist das mit Salat/Gemüse?
	ist das mit zalaat/germewser?
Do you have a children's menu?	Haben Sie einen Kinderteller?
	haaben zee I-nen kinnderteller?
Do you have any vegetarian dishes?	Haben Sie vegetarische Gerichte?
	haaben zee vegetaarisher gerishter?
I'd like my steak ...	Ich möchte mein Steak ...
	ish murshter myn shtaik...
...rare	blutig
	blootig
...medium	halbdurch
	halp-doorsh
...well done	durchgebraten
	doorsh-geerbraaten
I'm not allowed to eat...	Ich darf...nicht essen
	ish daarf...nisht essen
...eggs	...Eier
	I-er

...fat	...Fett *fet*
...flour	...Mehl *mail*
...sugar	....Zucker *tsooker*
...nuts	...Nüsse *newsser*
We'd all/ both like	Wir möchten alle/beide... *veer murshten aler/ byder...*
I'd like the menu at 30 Euros/ the dish of the day	Ich hätte gern das Menü zu dreißig Euro/das Tagesgericht *ish hetter gairn das menew tsoo drysig oyroh/das taagesgerisht*
That's for him/ her/ me	Das ist für ihn/sie/mich *das ist fewr een/zee/ mish*
The same for me, please	Das gleiche für mich, bitte *das glysher fewr mish bitter*
Could I have...instead?	Kann ich statt dessen...haben? *kan ish shtat dessen...haaben?*
Please may I have...?	Kann ich bitte...haben? *kan ish bitter...haaben?*
...some more	...etwas mehr *etvas mair*
...some (more) bread	...(noch) etwas Brot *(nokh) etvas broht*
...some (more) butter	...(noch) etwas Butter *(nokh) etvas booter*
...a (-nother) pot of coffee	...(noch) ein Kännchen Kaffee *(nokh) I-n kenshen kafai*
...a (-nother) cup of tea	...(noch) eine Tasse Tee *(nokh) I-ner tasser tai*
...a (-nother) glass of wine	...(noch) ein Glas Wein *(nokh) I-n glaas vyn*

...a (-nother) portion of...

...(noch) eine Portion...
(nokh) I-ner portsiohn...

No more, thank you

Nichts mehr, danke
nishts mair, danker

PROBLEMS & QUERIES

I ordered...

Ich habe...bestellt
ish haaber...bershtelt

We've been waiting for
20 minutes

Wir warten schon seit zwanzig
Minuten
*veer vaarten shohn zyt tsvantsig
minooten*

May I have a (-nother)...

Kann ich...haben?
kan ish...haaben?

...fork

...eine (andere) Gabel
I-ner (anderer) gaabel

...glass

...ein (anderes) Glas
I-n (anderes) glaas

...knife

...ein (anderes) Messer
I-n (anderes) messer

...spoon

...einen (anderen) Löffel...
I-nen (anderen) lurfel

...plate

...einen Teller
I-nen teller

This isn't clean

Das ist nicht sauber
das ist nisht zowber

This is...

Das ist...
das ist...

...burnt

...angebrannt
angerbrant

...cold

...kalt
kalt

...not fresh

...nicht frisch
nisht frisch

...overcooked

...verkocht
fairkokht

...too salty/ sweet

...zu salzig/süß
tsoo zaltsig/zewss

...underdone

...nicht gar
nisht gaar

PAYING THE BILL

I'd like to pay, please

Ich möchte zahlen, bitte
ish murshter tsaalen, bitter

We're paying together/
separately

Wir bezahlen zusammen/
getrennt
*veer bertsaalen tsoozammen/
gertrent*

There seems to be a mistake
in the bill

Ich glaube, Sie haben sich
verrechnet
*ish glowber, zee haaben zish
fairekhnet*

What is this amount for?

Wofür steht dieser Betrag?
*vohfewr stait deezer
bertraag?*

Does that include service?

Ist das mit Bedienung?
ist das mit berdeenoong?

Do you accept traveller's
cheques/ credit cards?

Nehmen Sie Reiseschecks/
Kreditkarten?
*naimen zee ryzer-sheks/
kredeet-kaarten?*

I don't have enough cash

Ich habe nicht genug in bar
*ish haaber nisht gernoog in
baar*

You've given me the
wrong change

Sie haben mir falsch
herausgegeben
*zee haaben meer falsch
hairowsgergaiben*

In restaurants, the service charge is usually included in the bill, although you may of course leave a little extra by rounding up the amount if you were especially pleased by the service you received.

| Keep the change | Stimmt so
shtimmt zoh |
| May I have a receipt? | Kann ich eine Quittung haben bitte?
kan ish I-ner kvittoong haaben bitter? |

You may hear

Bitte schön? *bitter shurn?*	} What would you like?
Was darf es sein? *vas darf es zyn?*	
Was möchten Sie? *vas murshten zee?*	

| Haben Sie schon gewählt?
haaben zee shohn gervailt? | }
Have you decided yet? |
| Haben Sie etwas ausgesucht?
haaben zee etvas awsgezookht? | |

Sonst noch etwas? *zonst nokh etvas?*	Anything else?
...haben wir nicht mehr *haaben veer nisht mair*	We haven't any more...
Möchten Sie einen Nachtisch? *murshten zee I-nen nakh-tish?*	Would you like a dessert?
Guten Appetit! *gooten appeteet!*	Enjoy your meal!
Hat es Ihnen geschmeckt? *hat ess eenen gershmeckt?*	Did you enjoy that?

You may see:

Hauptgerichte	main courses
hausgemacht	home-made
Imbisse	snacks

Im Preis inbegriffen	included in the price
Inklusive Bedienung und Mehrwertsteuer	service and VAT included
Mit Beilage	with salad or vegetables
Nachspeisen	desserts
Nur auf Bestellung	to order only
Spezialität des Hauses	speciality of the house
Tagesgedeck/Tagesmenü	set menu of the day
Tagesgericht	dish of the day

NON-ALCOHOLIC DRINKS

I'd like a/an...	Ich möchte… *ish murshter…*
...apple juice	...einen Apfelsaft *I-nen apfelzaft*
...blackcurrant juice	...einen Johannisbeersaft *I-nen Yohanisbairzaft*
...chocolate	...eine Schokolade *I-ner shokolaader*
...coffee	...einen Kaffee *I-nen kafai*
...Coke	...eine Cola *I-ner kohla*
...fruit juice	...einen Fruchtsaft *I-nen frookhtzaft*
...lemonade	...eine Limonade *I-ner limonaader*
...fizzy/ still mineral water	...ein Mineralwasser mit/ohne Kohlensäure *I-n mineraalvasser mit/ohner kohlenzoyrer*
...orange juice	...einen Orangensaft *I-nen oranjenzaft*

...tea   ...einen Tee
I-nen tai

...herb tea   ...einen Kräutertee
I-nen kroytertai

...tomato juice   ...einen Tomatensaft
I-nen tomaatenzaft

...tonic water   ...ein Tonic
I-n tonik

a cup   eine Tasse
I-ner tasser

a pot (holds about 2 cups)   ein Kännchen
I-n kenshen

a black coffee   einen schwarzen Kaffee
I-nen shvaartsen kafai

with cream   mit Sahne
mit zaaner

with milk   mit Milch
mit milsh

decaffeinated   koffeinfrei
koffe-eenfry

espresso   einen Espresso
I-nen espressoh

with lemon   mit Zitrone
mit tsitrohner

BEER

I'd like...   Ich möchte...
ish murshter

...a glass of...   ...ein Glas...
I-n glaas...

...two glasses of...   ...zwei Glas...
tsvy glaas...

...a bottle of...   ...eine Flasche...
I-ner flasher...

Tea is served without milk unless requested.

...two bottles of...	...zwei Flaschen... *tsvy flashen...*
...a tankard (litre)...	...eine Maß... *I-ner maas...*
...another beer, please	...noch ein Bier, bitte *nokh I-n beer bitter*

You may hear:

Altbier *altbeer*	a top-fermented, dark beer
Bier *beer*	beer
Bockbier/ Doppelbock *bokbeer/ doppelbok*	[types of] strong beer
Ein Dunkles *I-n doonkles*	a dark beer
Ein Helles *I-n helles*	a light-coloured beer
Malzbier *maltsbeer*	dark, sweet, low in alcohol
Märzen *mairtsen*	a strong, light beer
Pils/ Pilsner *pils/ pilsner*	like lager – the most common type of beer
...vom Fass *fom fass*	draught
Weißbier/ Weizenbier *vysbeer/ vytsenbeer*	a pale, fizzy beer made from wheat

Almost every town in Germany has its brewery, and there are dozens of types of beer, some brewed only at particular times of the year.

WINE

• Germany, Austria and Switzerland all produce wine. If you are in or near a wine-producing region, all pubs and restaurants will stock locally-produced wines, although you may be able to buy wines from other parts of Europe too.

The flabby, over-sweetened *Liebfraumilch* and *Hock* which are often the only German wines available in most British supermarkets and off-licences are unknown in Germany.

I'd like...	Ich möchte... *ish murshter*
... a glass of...	...ein Glas... *I-n glaas...*
...a bottle of...	...eine Flasche... *I-ner flasher...*
...red wine	...Rotwein *rohtvyn*
...white wine	...Weißwein *vysvyn*
...rosé	...Rosé *rohzay*
...sparkling wine/ champagne	...Sekt *zekt*
...white wine with soda/ mineral water	...eine Schorle *I-ner shorler*

QUALITY AND FLAVOUR

crisp	frisch/ herb *frish/ hairp*
dry	trocken *trocken*
fruity	fruchtig *frookhtig*

In pubs, the waiter or waitress will often mark your beermat each time you order a drink – you pay at the end of the evening. Almost all pubs have a waiter service, and it is normal to drink sitting down. No-one stands at the bar.

sweet	süß *zewss*	
light	leicht *lysht*	
full-bodied	vollmundig *follmoondig*	
table-wine/ 'plonk'	Tafelwein *taafelvyn*	

• The phrase 'Aus den Ländern der EU' may be included on the label. This indicates that most of the contents of the bottle are from other European countries; these wines are usually of very poor quality.

QbA *koo bai aa*	(Qualitätswein aus den bestimmten Anbaugebieten)	a blended wine from a certified region e.g. Mosel, Rhein
QmP *koo em pai*	(Qualitätswein mit Prädikat)	a quality wine with a title
	Kabinett *kabinett*	high quality
	Spätlese *shpaitlaizer*	late vintage
	Auslese *owslaizer*	late vintage from specially selected grapes
	Beerenauslese *bairen-owslaizer*	made from selected over-ripe grapes
	Trockenbeerenauslese *trokenbairen-owslaizer*	made from grapes so over-ripe they are like raisins.
	Eiswein *I-svyn*	an intense wine made from frozen grapes

You could also try *Schillerwein*, which is made by fermenting white and red grapes together, or *Weißherbst*, which is a very light wine made from bluish-skinned grapes.

• The QmP titles indicate stages, not of increasing quality, but of increasing intensity and, usually, sweetness. With most savoury foods, a *Kabinett* or dry *(trocken) Spätlese* is recommended.

• A *Qualitätswein* (quality wine) will also have the name of the village and the vineyard where it was produced:

e.g. *Eltviller Langenstück – Eltville* is the village, *Langenstück* is the vineyard.

MAIN GRAPE VARIETIES

<u>White wines</u>

Riesling *reezling*	fresh; older wines elegant
Silvaner *zilvaaner*	gentle flavour
Müller-Thurgau *mewler-toorgow*	fruity, rounded
Gewürztraminer *gervewrts-trameener*	tending to spicy flavour

<u>Red wines</u>

Spätburgunder *shpaitboorgoonder*	the *pinot noir*; can be quite full-bodied in a good year
Lemberger *lembuirger*	can be dry, full-bodied, but varies according to vineyard (SW Germany only)
Portugieser *portoogeezer*	rounded flavour
Trollinger *trolinger*	fresh and fruity (SW Germany only)

OTHER ALCOHOLIC DRINKS

I'd like a/ an/ some...	Ich möchte... *ish murshter...*
...brandy	...einen Weinbrand *I-nen vynbrant*

...cider	...einen Apfelwein/ Apfelmost *I-nen apfelvyn/ apfelmosst*
...cognac	...einen Kognak *I-nen konyak*
...gin	...einen Gin *I-nen jin*

• **Doornkaat** *(doornkaat)* and **Steinhäger** *(shtynhaiger)* are the two best-known varieties of *Schnapps*.

...liqueur	...einen Likör *I-nen likur*
...port	...einen Portwein *I-nen portvyn*
...rum	...einen Rum *I-nen room*
...sherry	...einen Sherry *I-nen sherri*
...vermouth	...einen Wermut *I-nen vairmut*
...vodka	...einen Wodka *I-nen vodka*
...whisky	...einen Whisky *I-nen viskee*
neat (straight)	pur *poor*
with ice (on the rocks)	mit Eis *mit I-s*

German specialities include *Geist* (a clear spirit made from fruit e.g. *Kirschgeist* is the cherry variety), *Korn* (corn brandy) and *Schnapps* (a strong, clear brandy).

WHAT'S ON THE MENU?

The immense variety of German regional cookery makes it impossible to do much more here than to list the main vocabulary to be found on menus. Most menus explain what goes into each dish.

Ananas	*ananas*	pineapple
Apfel	*apfel*	apple
Apfelsine	*apfelzeener*	orange
Aprikose	*aprikohze*	apricot
Artischocken	*aartishohken*	artichokes
Auberginen	*ohberjeenen*	aubergines
Auflauf	*owflowf*	casserole
Austern	*owstern*	oysters
Back-	*bak-*	roasted, baked
Backpflaumen	*bak-pflowmen*	prunes
Baiser	*bezai*	meringue
Banane	*banaaner*	banana
Bauernfrühstück	*bowern-frewstewck*	potato and bacon omelette
Bedienung	*berdeenoong*	service
Beilage	*by-laager*	side-dish (vegetable or salad)
Berliner	*berleener*	jam doughnut
Birne	*beerner*	pear
Blumenkohl	*bloomen-kohl*	cauliflower
Blutwurst	*bloot-voorst*	black pudding
Bockwurst	*bokvoorst*	frankfurter
Bohnen	*bohnen*	beans
grüne	*grewner*	green (French)
weiße	*vysser*	white (haricot)
Brat-	*braat*	roasted
Braten	*braaten*	roast meat

Bratwurst	*braatvoorst*	fried sausage
Brokkoli	*brokolee*	broccoli
Brombeeren	*brombeeren*	blackberries
Brot	*broht*	bread
Brötchen	*brurtshen*	bread roll
Champignons	*shampinyongs*	mushrooms
Currywurst	*curry-voorst*	sausage with curry sauce
Datteln	*datteln*	dates
Dorsch	*dorsh*	cod
Eier	*I-er*	eggs
mit Einlage	*mit I-nlaager*	egg, vegetables, etc. added to a clear soup
Eintopf	*I-ntopf*	stew
Eisbecher	*I-sbesher*	sundae/ice cream
englisch	*ennglish*	rare (meat)
Ente	*enter*	duck
Erbsen	*airbzen*	peas
Erdbeeren	*airdbairen*	strawberries
Erdnüsse	*airdnewsser*	peanuts
Essig	*essig*	vinegar
Feigen	*fugen*	figs
Feldsalat	*felt-salaat*	lamb's lettuce
Fenchel	*fenshel*	fennel
Filet	*filai*	fillet
Fisch	*fish*	fish

Fleischkäse	*flush-kaiser*	meat loaf
Fleischpastete	*flush-pastaiter*	pâté
Forelle	*foreller*	trout
Frikadelle	*frickadeller*	meat rissole
Frühlingsrolle	*frewlings-roller*	spring roll
Gans	*gans*	goose
Garnelen	*gaarnailen*	prawns
garniert	*gaarneert*	garnished
Gebäck	*gerbek*	cakes/pastries/biscuits
gebacken	*gerbaken*	baked
gemischter Salat	*germishter zalaat*	mixed salad
Gemüse	*germewser*	vegetables
geräuchert	*geroyshert*	smoked
gebraten	*gerbraaten*	roasted
gedämpft	*gerdempft*	steamed
Geflügel	*gerflewgel*	poultry
gefüllt	*gerfewlt*	stuffed
gegrillt	*gergrillt*	grilled
gehackt	*gerhakt*	chopped/minced
gekocht	*gerkokht*	cooked/boiled
Getränke	*gertrenker*	drinks
gewürzt	*gervewrtst*	flavoured with spices
Grießklößchen	*grees-klursshen*	semolina dumplings
grüner Salat	*grewner zalaat*	green salad
Gurken	*goorken*	cucumbers/gherkins

Hackfleisch	*hakflysh*	minced meat
Hähnchen	*hainshen*	chicken
Haselnüsse	*haazelnewsser*	hazelnuts
Hauptgerichte	*howpt-gerishter*	main courses
Hauptspeisen	*howpt-spyzern*	main courses
hausgemacht	*hows-germakht*	home-made
Hering	*hairing*	herring
Himbeeren	*himbairen*	raspberries
Hirschmedaillons	*heersh-medayohngs*	venison fillets
Honig	*hohnig*	honey
Huhn	*hoon*	chicken
Hühnerbrühe	*hewnerbrewer*	chicken broth
Hummer	*hoomer*	lobster
Kaffee	*kafai*	coffee
Kartoffelpuffer	*kaartoffel-puffer*	potato fritters
Käse	*kaiser*	cheese
Käsekuchen	*kaizer-kookhen*	cheesecake
Kassler	*kassler*	braised smoked pork chop
Kirschen	*keershen*	cherries
Kokosnuss	*kohkosnoos*	coconut
Königsberger Klopse	*kurnigsbairger klopser*	meat balls with caper sauce
Kraftbrühe	*krafft-brewer*	beef soup
Kuchen	*kookhen*	cake/gateau
Ingwer	*ingver*	ginger

Jäger	*Yaiger*	with a spicy sauce
Johannisbeeren	*Yohannis-bairen*	currants
rote	*rohter*	red
schwarze	*schvaartser*	black
Kabeljau	*kaabelYow*	cod
Kalb (-fleisch)	*kalp (-flysh)*	veal
Kalte Platte	*kalter platter*	selection of cold meats
Kaninchen	*kaneenshen*	rabbit
Karotten	*karotten*	carrots
Kartoffeln	*kaartoffeln*	potatoes
Kartoffelbrei	*kaartofferlbr-I*	mashed potatoes
Klösschen	*klursshen*	dumplings
Knackwurst	*knakvoorst*	type of Frankfurter
Knoblauch	*knohb-lowkh*	garlic
Kohl	*kohl*	cabbage
Kopfsalat	*kopfzalaat*	lettuce
Kotelett	*kohtelet*	chop/cutlet
Krabben	*krabben*	shrimps/prawns
Kräuter	*kroyter*	herbs
Krebs	*krebz*	crab
Lachs	*lukhs*	salmon
Lamm (-fleisch)	*lam (-flysh)*	lamb
Lauch	*lowkh*	leek
Leber	*laiber*	liver
Leipziger Allerlei	*lyptsiger alerly*	mixed vegetables

Limone	*lim<u>oh</u>ner*	lime
Linsen	*l<u>i</u>nzen*	lentils
Mais	*mys*	sweetcorn
Makrele	*makr<u>ai</u>ler*	mackerel
Mandarine	*mandar<u>ee</u>ner*	mandarin/tangerine
Mandeln	*m<u>a</u>ndeln*	almonds
Medaillons	*meday<u>oh</u>ngs*	small fillets of meat
Meeresfrüchte	*m<u>ai</u>res-frewshter*	seafood
Meerrettichsoße	*m<u>ai</u>rrettish-sohsser*	horseradish sauce
Melone	*mel<u>oh</u>ner*	melon
zum Mitnehmen	*tsoom m<u>i</u>tnaimen*	to take away
Möhren	*m<u>u</u>ren*	carrots
Mohrrüben	*m<u>oh</u>rewben*	carrots
Mokka	*m<u>o</u>ka*	coffee
Mus	*moos*	puree
MwSt (Mehrwertsteuer)	*m<u>ai</u>r-vairt-stoyer*	VAT
Nachspeisen	*n<u>a</u>kh-shpyzen*	desserts
Nieren	*n<u>ee</u>ren*	kidneys
Nudeln	*n<u>oo</u>deln*	noodles
Nüsse	*n<u>ew</u>sser*	nuts
Obst	*ohbst*	fruit
Oliven	*ol<u>ee</u>ven*	olives
Olivenöl	*ol<u>ee</u>ven-url*	olive oil
Orange	*or<u>o</u>njer*	orange
Palatschinken	*palaat-sh<u>i</u>nken*	stuffed pancakes

Pampelmuse	*pampelmoozer*	grapefruit
paniert	*paneert*	cooked in bread crumbs
Paprikaschoten	*papreeka-shohten*	green peppers
Pellkartoffeln	*pell-kaartoffeln*	potatoes boiled in their jackets
Pfannkuchen	*pfankookhen*	pancake
Pfeffer	*pfeffer*	pepper
Pfirsich	*pfeerzish*	peach
Pflaumen	*pflowmen*	plums
Pilze	*piltser*	mushrooms
Platte	*platter*	platter, selection
Pommes frites	*pom frit*	chips (french fries)
Porree	*porai*	leek
Poularde	*poolaard*	chicken
Pute	*pooter*	turkey
Pumpernickel	*poompernickel*	dark rye bread
Püree	*pewrai*	puree
Quark	*kvaark*	curd cheese
Rahm	*raam*	cream
Radieschen	*radeeshen*	radishes
Räucherlachs	*roykher-lakhs*	smoked salmon
Reh	*rai*	venison
Reis	*rys*	rice
Rhabarber	*rabaarber*	rhubarb
Rind (-fleisch)	*rint (-flysh)*	beef

Rippchen	*ripshen*	spare ribs
Rohschinken	*roh-shinken*	cured ham
Rosenkohl	*rohzenkohl*	brussels sprouts
Rosinen	*rohzeenen*	raisins
Rostbraten	*rostbraaten*	roast
rote Beete	*rohte baite*	beetroot
Rotkohl	*rohtkohl*	red cabbage
Russische Eier	*roosisher I-er*	eggs/mayonnaise
mit/ohne Sahne	*mit/ohner zaaner*	with/without cream
Salat	*zalaat*	salad
Salatsoße	*salaat-sohser*	salad dressing
Salz	*zalts*	salt
Salzkartoffeln	*zalts-kaartoffeln*	boiled potatoes
Sardinen	*zaardeenen*	sardines
Sauerbraten	*zower-braaten*	roast marinated beef
scharf	*shaarf*	hot/highly seasoned
Schaschlik	*shashlik*	kebab
Schinken	*shinken*	ham
Schlachtplatte	*shlakhtplatter*	selection of cold meats and sausages
Schlagsahne	*shlaagzaaner*	whipped cream
Schnitzel	*shnitzel*	escalope
Schokolade	*shokohlaader*	chocolate
Scholle	*sholler*	plaice
Schwein (-efleisch)	*shvyner (-flysh)*	pork
Seezunge	*zai-tsoonger*	sole

Semmelknödel	*zemmelknurdel*	bread dumplings
Senf	*zenf*	mustard
Soße	*sohsser*	sauce
Spargel	*shpaargel*	asparagus
Speck	*shpek*	bacon
Speisekarte	*shpyzer-kaarter*	menu
Spinat	*shpinaat*	spinach
Stangensellerie	*shtangern-zeleree*	celery
Strammer Max	*shtrammer max*	ham and fried egg on bread
Suppe	*zooper*	soup
süß-sauer	*zews-zower*	sweet and sour
Süßspeisen	*zewss-shpyzern*	desserts
Tagesgericht	*taages-gerisht*	dish of the day
Tagesmenü	*taages-menew*	menu of the day
Teig	*tyg*	pastry
Teigwaren	*tyg-vaaren*	pasta
Thunfisch	*toonfish*	tuna
Tomaten	*tomaaten*	tomatoes
Torte	*torter*	gâteau/flan
Truthahn	*troothaan*	turkey
überbacken	*ewberbacken*	au gratin, lightly grilled
vegetarisch	*vegetaarish*	vegetarian
vom Grill	*fomm grill*	grilled
Vorspeisen	*fohr-shpyzen*	starters, hors d'oeuvre
Walnuss	*valnooss*	walnut

Wassermelone	*vassermelohner*	watermelon
Weintrauben	*vyntrowben*	grapes
Weißkohl	*vyskohl*	white cabbage
Wiener Schnitzel	*veener shnitzel*	veal escalope
Wild	*vilt*	game/venison
würzig	*vewrtsig*	spicy
Wurstplatte	*voorstplatter*	selection of cold sausage
Würze	*vewrtser*	seasoning/spice
Zander	*tsander*	pike-perch, zander
Zitrone	*tsitrohner*	lemon
Zucchini	*tsookhini*	courgettes
Zucker	*tsooker*	sugar
Zwiebeln	*tsveebeln*	onions
Zwetschgen	*tsvechgen*	plums
Zwiebelkuchen	*tsveebel-kookhen*	onion tart

ENTERTAINMENT AND SPORT

• You can find out what's on from the tourist office, or from the local newspaper.

• Foreign films are usually dubbed into German rather than sub-titled.

• The German-speaking countries are well-known for their winter sports facilities. Germany has resorts not only in the Alps, but also in the Black Forest (*Schwarzwald*), and the Harz Mountains. Both downhill (*Abfahrtslauf*) and cross-country skiing (*Langlauf*) are popular.

Many more towns than in Britain have a theatre and concert hall, and opera or ballet companies. Booking is usually advisable.

WHAT'S ON?

What is there to do this evening?
Was kann man heute Abend unternehmen?
vas kan man hoyter aabent oonter-naimen?

I'm interested in...
Ich interessiere mich für...
ish interesseerer mish fewr...

...classical music
...klassische Musik
klassisher moozeek

...pop music
...Popmusik
popmoozeek

...jazz
...Jazz
jaz

...folk music
...Volksmusik
Folks-moozeek

...films
...Filme
filmer

I'd like to go...
Ich möchte...gehen
ish murshter...gai-en

...to the cinema
...ins Kino...
ins keeno...

...to a club
...in eine Disko...
in I-ner Diskoh...

...to a nightclub
...in einen Nachtclub...
in I-nen nakht-kloob...

...to the theatre
...ins Theater...
ins tai-aater...

...to a concert
...in ein Konzert...
in I-n kontsairt...

...to the opera
...in die Oper...
in dee ohper...

...the ballet	...ins Ballett... *ins balett...*
Can you recommend a club/ a nightclub?	Können Sie eine Disko/ einen Nachtclub empfehlen? *kurnen zee I-ner diskoh/I-nen nakht-kloob empfailen?*
Are there any tickets for this evening/ tomorrow?	Gibt es Karten für heute Abend/morgen? *gipt es kaarten fewr hoyter aabent/ morgen?*
How much are the tickets?	Was kosten die Karten? *vas kosten dee kaarten?*
When does it begin?	Wann beginnt es? *van bergint es?*
When does it end?	Wann ist es zu Ende? *van ist es tsoo ender?*
I'd like 1/ 2 tickets...	Ich möchte eine Karte/ 2 Karten... *ish murshter I-ner kaarter/ tsvy kaarten...*
...for this evening	...für heute Abend *fewr hoyter aabent*
...for tomorrow	...für morgen *fewr mohrgen*
...in the circle/ stalls	...im Rang/Parkett *im rang/parket*

You may hear:

Ich empfehle... *Ish empfailer...*	I recommend...
Die Plätze sind ausverkauft *dee pletser zint owsfairkowft*	The tickets are sold out
Es gibt nur noch ein paar Plätze *Es gipt noor nokh I-n paar pletser*	There are just a few tickets left

CONCERTS, OPERA, BALLET

What's being played?

Was wird gespielt?
vas veert gershpeelt?

Which opera/ ballet is
being performed?

Welche Oper/ welches Ballet
wird aufgeführt?
*velsher ohper/ velshes balett veert
owf-gerfewrt?*

Who's the soloist/ conductor?

Wer ist der Solist/ Dirigent?
vair ist dair zolist/ dirigent?

When is the interval?

Wann ist die Pause?
van ist dee powzer?

How long does the interval last?

Wie lange dauert die Pause?
vee langer dowert dee powzer?

CINEMAS AND THEATRES

What's on at the cinema?

Was läuft im Kino?
vas loyft im keenoh?

What's on at the theatre?

Was wird im Theater aufgeführt?
*vas veert im tai-aarter
owfgerfewrt?*

What sort of film/ play is it?

Was für ein Film/ Stück ist es?
vas fewr I-n film/ shtewk ist es?

Is it...?

Ist es...?
ist es...?

...a comedy

...eine Komödie
I-ner kommurdi-er

...a musical

...ein Musical
I-n 'musical'

...a horror film

...ein Horrorfilm
I-n horohrfilm

...a thriller

...ein Krimi
I-n krimmi

...a German film	...ein deutscher Film *I-n doycher film*
...subtitled	...mit Untertiteln *mit oonter-teetln*
...dubbed	...synchronisiert *zewn-khronizeert*
Who is in it?	Wer sind die Schauspieler? *vair zint dee show-shpeeler?*
Who wrote the play?	Wer hat das Stück geschrieben? *vair hat das shtewk gershreeben?*
Where is the cloakroom?	Wo ist die Garderobe? *voh ist dee gaarder-rohber?*
May I have a programme?	Kann ich bitte ein Programm haben? *kan ish bitter I-n prohgram haaben?*

You may see:

Veranstaltungen	Events
Vorverkauf (-sstelle)	Advance booking (-office)
heute	Today
ausverkauft	Sold out
Letzte Vorstellung	Last showing (of film)
Nächste Aufführung	Next performance (of play, etc.)

RELAXING WITH FRIENDS

Would you like to come over...?	Möchtest du...zu uns kommen? *murshtest doo...tsoo oons kommen?*
...this evening...	...heute Abend... *hoyter aabent...*

...tomorrow...	...morgen... *mohrgen...*
...on Saturday...	...am Samstag... *am zamztaag...*
...for a glass of wine/beer...	...auf ein Glas Wein/Bier... *owf I-n glaas vyn/beer...*
...for lunch...	...zum Mittagessen... *tsoom mitaag-essen...*
...for dinner...	...zum Abendessen... *tsoom aabentessen...*
...to a party...	...auf eine Party... *owf I-ner partee...*
At what time?	Um wie viel Uhr? *oom veefeel oor?*
At eight	Um acht *oom akht*
At about nine	Gegen neun *gaigen noyn*
I'm afraid we must leave now	Leider müssen wir jetzt gehen *lyder mewsen veer Yetst gai-en*
It was lovely	Es war schön *es vaar shurn*
I've enjoyed it!	Es hat mir Spaß gemacht! *es hat meer shpass germakht!*

SPORT

I'd like to see...	Ich möchte...sehen *ish murshter...sai-en*
...a football match...	...ein Fußballspiel... *I-n foosbal-shpeel...*
...a tennis match...	...ein Tennisspiel... *I-n tennis-shpeel...*

...some horse-racing	...ein Pferderennen... *I-n pfairder-rennen...*
Is there ... near here?	Gibt es ... in der Nähe? *gipt es... in dair nai-er?*
...a golf course...	...einen Golfplatz... *I-nen golf-plats...*
...a tennis course...	...einen Tennisplatz... *I-nen tennis-plats...*
...a swimming pool...	...ein Schwimmbad... *I-n shvimmbaat...*
Do you have to be a member?	Muss man Mitglied sein? *Mooss man mitgleet zyn?*
Who's playing?	Wer spielt? *vair shpeelt?*
When does it start?	Wann beginnt es? *van berginnt es?*
How much are the tickets?	Was kostet der Eintritt? *vas kostet dair I-ntrit?*
Can you get me a ticket?	Können Sie mir eine Karte besorgen? *kurnen zee meer I-ner kaarter berzohrgen?*
Can you get us some tickets?	Können Sie uns Karten besorgen? *kurnen zee oons kaarten berzohrgen?*
What are the opening times?	Wie sind die Öffnungszeiten? *vee zint dee urfnoongstsyten?*
Is it an open-air or an indoor pool?	Ist es ein Freibad oder ein Hallenbad? *ist es I-n frybaat ohder I-n hallenbaat?*
Is it heated?	Ist es geheizt? *ist es gerhytst?*

Can one swim in the lake/ river?	Kann man im See/Fluss schwimmen? *kan man im zai/ floos shvimmen?*
Is there any fishing near here?	Kann man hier in der Nähe angeln? *kan man heer in dair nai-er angeln?*
Do I need a fishing permit?	Braucht man einen Angelschein? *browkht man I-nen angelshyn?*
How do I get a permit?	Wie bekomme ich einen Schein? *vee berkommer ish I-nen shyn?*
I'd like to play...	Ich möchte...spielen *ish murshter...shpeelen*
Where can we play...?	Wo können wir...spielen? *vo kurnen veer...shpeelen?*
Can I play...?	Kann ich...spielen? *kan ish...shpeelen?*
...golf...	...Golf... *golf...*
...tennis...	...Tennis... *tennis...*
...football...	...Fußball... *foosbal...*
What does it cost per...?	Was kostet es pro...? *vas kostet es pro...?*
...day	...Tag *taag*
...game/ round	...Spiel *shpeel*
...hour	...Stunde *shtoonder*

Can I hire...?	Kann ich....mieten? *kan ish...meeten?*
I'd like to hire...	Ich möchte...mieten *ish murshter...meeten*
Where can I hire...?	Wo kann ich...mieten? *vo kan ish...meeten?*
...a bicycle...	...ein Fahrrad... *I-n faarraat...*
...a boat...	...ein Boot... *I-n boot...*
...equipment...	...eine Ausrüstung... *I-ner owsrewstoong...*
...a windsurf board...	...ein Windsurfbrett... *I-n vintsoorf-brett...*

THE BEACH

Can you recommend a beach?	Können Sie einen Strand empfehlen? *kurnen zee I-nen shtrant empfailen?*
Is it safe for children?	Ist es für Kinder ungefährlich? *ist es fewr kinnder oon-gerfairlish?*
Is it safe for swimming?	Kann man hier ohne Gefahr schwimmen? *kan man heer ohner gerfaar schvimmen?*
Is there a lifeguard?	Gibt es eine Strandwache? *gipt es I-ner shtrant-vakher?*
When is the high tide/ low tide?	Wann ist Flut/ Ebbe? *van ist floot/ebber?*
I want to hire...	Ich möchte...mieten *ish murshter...meeten*

The coasts of Germany, facing the North Sea and the Baltic, have many miles of sandy beaches and dunes. These can be rather windy, so it is worth hiring a *Strandkorb*, a wicker chair with a hood.

...a deck-chair...	...einen Liegestuhl...
	I-nen leeger-shtool...
...a sailing boat...	...ein Segelboot...
	I-nen saigel-boot...
...a sunshade...	...einen Sonnenschirm...
	I-nen zonnen-sheerm...
...a surfboard...	...ein Surfbrett...
	I-n zoorf-bret...

You may hear:

Es ist (nicht) gefährlich	It's (not) dangerous
es ist (nisht) gerfairlish	

You may see:

Angeln verboten	No fishing
Baden verboten	No swimming
Bootsverleih	Boat hire
Eisstadion	Ice rink
Fahrradweg	Cycle path
FKK-Strand	Nudist beach
Freibad	Open-air swimming pool
Gefahr	Danger
Hallenbad	Indoor swimming pool
Lawinengefahr	Danger of avalanches
Privatstrand	Private beach
Tennisplätze	Tennis courts
Zuschauer	Spectators
Zum Skilift	To the skilift

WINTER SPORTS

I want to hire...	Ich möchte...mieten *ish murshter...meeten*
...a complete set of ski equipment...	...eine komplette Skiausrüstung... *I-ner kompletter shee-owsrewstoong...*
...skis...	...Skier... *shee-er...*
...ski boots...	...Skistiefel... *shee-shteeferl...*
Can I take skiing lessons?	Kann ich Skiunterricht nehmen? *kan ish shee-oonterisht naimen?*
Are there...?	Gibt es...? *gipt es...?*
...ski-runs for beginners	...Skipisten für Anfänger *shee-peesten fewr anfenger*
...ski-runs for advanced skiers	...Skipisten für Fortgeschrittene *sheepeesten fewr fortgershrittener*
...ski-lifts	...Skilifte *sheelifter*
How much does a daily/ weekly lift pass cost?	Was kostet eine Tageskarte/ Wochenkarte für den Lift? *vas kostet I-ner taages- karter/vokhen-kaarter fewr dain lift?*
What are the snow conditions like?	Wie sind die Schneeverhältnisse? *vee zint dee shnai-fairheltnisser?*

HEALTH

When travelling to Switzerland, you need to take out health insurance.

Chemists (*Apotheke*) will give advice and every town has its duty chemist open all night and at the weekend (see page 133).

For emergency telephone numbers, see page 154.

AT THE DOCTOR'S

My...hurts	...tut mir weh *toot meer vai*
...arm...	Der Arm... *dair aarm...*

As Germany and Austria are in the European Union, UK visitors are entitled to free medical and dental treatment, even if they have no private holiday insurance (which is, in any case, a useful back-up). Full details are given in the booklet which accompanies the E111 form which you can get from any Post Office.

...back...	Der Rücken... *dair rewken...*
...chest...	Die Brust... *dee broost...*
...eye...	Das Auge... *das owger...*
...head...	Der Kopf... *dair kopf...*
...leg...	Das Bein... *das byn...*
...stomach...	Der Magen... *dair maagen...*
...neck...	Der Hals... *dair hals...*
...foot...	Der Fuss... *dair foos...*
I've been bitten (animal)	Ich bin gebissen worden *ish bin gerbissen worden*
I've been stung	Ich bin gestochen worden *ish bin gerstokhen worden*
He/ she is...	Er/sie... *air/zee*
...unconscious	...ist bewusstlos *ist bervoostlohss*
...bleeding	...blutet *blootet*
...seriously injured	...ist schwer verletzt *ist shvair fairletst*
I've got...	Ich habe... *ish haaber...*
...asthma	...Asthma *astma*

...a chest pain	...Brustschmerzen *br<u>oo</u>stshmairtsen*
...a cold	...eine Erkältung *<u>I</u>-ner airk<u>e</u>ltoong*
...a cough	...Husten *h<u>oo</u>sten*
...earache	...Ohrenschmerzen *<u>oh</u>ren-schmairtsen*
...something in my eye	...etwas in meinem Auge *etvas in m<u>y</u>nem <u>ow</u>ger*
...hayfever	...Heuschnupfen *h<u>oy</u>shnoopfen*
...a migraine	...Migräne *migr<u>ai</u>ner*
...period pains	...Menstruationsbeschwerden *menstroo-atsi<u>oh</u>ns-bershvairden*
...a rash	...einen Ausschlag *<u>I</u>-nen <u>ow</u>s-shlaag*
...a sore throat	...Halsschmerzen *h<u>a</u>ls-shmairtsen*
...sunstroke	...einen Sonnenstich *<u>I</u>-nen z<u>o</u>nnen-shtish*
Can you fetch a doctor?	Können Sie einen Arzt holen? *k<u>u</u>rnen zee <u>I</u>-nen <u>aa</u>rtst h<u>o</u>hlen?*
I feel faint/ sick	Ich fühle mich schwach/ schlecht *ish f<u>ew</u>ler mish shvakh/ schlesht*
I feel dizzy	Mir ist schwindelig *meer ist shv<u>i</u>nderlig*
I've got diarrhoea/ a temperature	Ich habe Durchfall/ Fieber *ish h<u>aa</u>ber d<u>oo</u>rshfall/ f<u>ee</u>ber*
I've been sick	Ich habe mich übergeben *ish h<u>aa</u>ber mish ewberg<u>ai</u>ben*

It hurts...	Es tut weh...
	es toot vai...
...all the time	...die ganze Zeit
	dee gantser tsyt
...when I do this	...wenn ich das mache
	ven ish das makher
I am...	Ich bin...
	ish bin...
...diabetic	...Diabetiker
	diabaitiker
...epileptic	...Epileptiker
	Epileptikker
...pregnant	...schwanger
	shvanger
...allergic to antibiotics/ penicillin	...allergisch gegen Antibiotika/ Penizillin
	alairgish gaigen antibiohtika/ penitsileen
I'm on the Pill	Ich nehme die Pille
	ish naimer dee piller
I had a heart attack	Ich hatte einen Herzinfarkt
	ish hatter I-nen hairtsinfaarkt
I need a prescription for...	Ich brauche ein Rezept für...
	ish browkher I-n retsept fewr...
Is it serious?	Ist es schlimm?
	ist es shlim?
Could you tell my family/ hotel?	Können Sie bitte meine Familie/ mein Hotel benachrichtigen?
	kurnen zee bitter myner fameelier/ myn hotel bernakhrishtigen?
I've been in pain...	Ich habe Schmerzen seit...
	ish haaber shmairtsen zyt...

...for several days

...einigen Tagen
I-nigen taagen

...since yesterday

...gestern
gestern

...since this morning

...heute morgen
hoyter mohrgen

...for a few hours

...einigen Stunden
I-nigen shtoonden

May I have a receipt for my insurance company?

Kann ich eine Quittung für meine Krankenkasse haben?
kan ish I-ner kvittoong fewr myner kranken-kasser haaben?

May I have a medical certificate?

Kann ich einen Krankenschein haben?
kan ish I-nen kranken-shyn haaben?

Could you sign this please?

Können Sie das bitte unterschreiben?
kurnen zee das bitter oonter-shryben?

You may see:

Alle Kassen	**All health insurance patients**
Arzt/Ärztin für... Allgemeinmedizin	**General Practitioner**
Facharzt/Fachärztin für...	**Specialist in...**
Krankenhaus/Klinik	**Hospital**
Krankenwagen	**Ambulance**
Medikament(e)	**medicine(s)**
Nach Vereinbarung	**By appointment**
Notarzt	**Emergency Doctor**
Sprechstunde	**surgery**

Untersuchung	check-up
Wartezimmer	waiting room

You may hear:

Ich gebe Ihnen…
ish gaiber eenen

I'll give you…

…eine Spritze
I-ner shpritser

…an injection

…einen Salbe
I-ner zalber

…some ointment

…ein Rezept
I-n retsept

…a prescription

…ein Schmerzmittel
I-n shmairtsmittel

…a painkiller

Wo tut es weh?
voh toot es vai?

Where does it hurt?

Wie lange geht es Ihnen
schon so?
*vee langer gait es eenen
shohn so?*

How long have you been
feeling like this?

Tief atmen, bitte
teef aatmen, bitter

Breathe deeply, please

Husten Sie, bitte
hoosten zee bitter

Cough, please

Sie müssen…Tage lang im
Bett bleiben
*zee mewssen…taager lang im
bet blyben*

You must stay in bed for…days

Sie müssen ins Krankenhaus
gehen
*zee mewssen ins krankenhows
gai-en*

You must go to hospital

Es ist…
es ist…

It's…

…eine Blinddarmentzündung
I-ner blint-darm-enttsewndoong

…appendicitis

…eine Gehirnerschütterung
I-ner gerheern-ershewtteroong

…concussion

…eine Grippe
I-ner gripper

…flu

…eine Lebensmittelvergiftung
I-ner laibenzmittel-fairgiftoong

…food poisoning

…eine Magenverstimmung
I-ner maagen-fairshtimmoong

…an stomach upset

…ein Sonnenstich
I-n zonnen-shtish

…sunstroke

…gebrochen
gerbrokhen

…broken/ fractured

…infiziert
infitseert

…infected

…verrenkt
fairrenkt

…dislocated

…verstaucht
fairshtowkht

…sprained

Sie sollten zum Arzt gehen
zee zollten tsoom aartst gehen

You'll need to see a doctor

Sie brauchen ein Rezept dafür
zee browkhen I-n Retsept dafewr

You need a prescription for that

Nehmen Sie jeweils … Tabletten
naimen zee yaivyls … tabletten

Take … tablets at a time

Einmal/zweimal täglich
I-nmaal/tsvymaal taiglish

Once/twice a day

vor/nach dem Essen
fohr/nakh daim essen

before/after meals

Was nehmen Sie sonst? *vas naimen zee zonst?*	What else do you take?
Sie müssen zum Röntgen gehen *zee mewssen tsoom rurntgen gai-en*	You'll need to have it x-rayed
Sie müssen operiert werden *zee mewssen operiert vairden*	You'll need to have an operation

AT THE DENTIST

I've got toothache	Ich habe Zahnschmerzen *ish haaber tsaan-shmairtsen*
Can you recommend a dentist?	Können Sie einen Zahnarzt empfehlen? *kurnen zee I-nen tsaan-artst empfailen?*
Can I make an appointment?	Kann ich einen Termin haben? *kan ish I-nen tairmeen haaben?*
It's urgent	Es ist dringend *es ist dringent*
I've lost a filling/ crown	Ich habe eine Plombe/ eine Krone verloren *ish haaber I-ner plomber/ I-ner krohner fairlohren*
It's this tooth	Es ist dieser Zahn *es ist deezer tsaan*
Can you give me an anaesthetic?	Können Sie mir eine Spritze geben? *kurnen zee meer I-ner spritzer gaiben?*
I've broken my denture	Ich habe meine Prothese zerbrochen *Ish haaber myner prohtaizer zerbrokhen*
Can you repair it?	Können Sie es reparieren? *kurnen zee es parpareeren?*

How long will it take?	Wie lange dauert es? *vee langer dowert es?*
I'm insured	Ich bin versichert *ish bin fairsishert*

You may hear:

Welcher Zahn tut Ihnen weh? *velsher tsaan toot eenen vai?*	Which tooth hurts?

SHOPPING AND SERVICES

• Opening times are as follows:

	Weekdays	*Saturdays*
Germany	8/9am to 6/6.30pm	8/9am to 12/2pm
Austria	8/9am to 6/6.30pm	8/9am to 12/2pm
Switzerland	8/9am to 6/6.30pm	8/9am to 4/5pm

• Some shops close for lunch.

• Bookshops and stationers are usually separate. Magazines and newspapers can be bought at news-stands and at many bookshops.

• Chemists (*Apotheke*) sell only medicines and health items. For toiletries, films etc, look for a *Drogerie*.

In Germany, shops stay open untill 6pm on the first Saturday of every month.
In Switzerland, shops are often closed on Monday morning.

SHOPPING

Where can I buy...?	Wo kann ich ... kaufen?
	voh kan ish ... kowfen?
I'm looking for...	Ich suche...
	ish zookher
I'm just looking	Ich sehe mich nur um
	ish sai-er mish noor oom
Can you help me?	Können Sie mir helfen?
	kurnen zee meer helfen?
Do you have any ...?	Haben Sie ...?
	haaben zee ...?
Where is the...?	Wo ist...?
	voh ist...?
...lift	...der Fahrstuhl
	dair faar-shtool
...escalator	...die Rolltreppe
	dee rol-trepper
...till/check-out	...die Kasse
	dee kasser
Where are the ...?	Wo finde ich...?
	voh finder ish...?
I saw it in the window	Ich habe es im Fenster gesehen
	ish haaber es im fenster gersai-en
That one/those	Das da/die da
	das daa/dee daa
Do you have any others?	Haben Sie noch andere?
	haaben zee nokh anderer?
Do you have any more?	Haben Sie noch mehr davon?
	haaben zee nokh mair daafon?
Do you have it in any other colours?	Haben Sie es in anderen Farben?
	haaben zee es in anderen faarben?

It's for a present	Es ist ein Geschenk *es is I-n gershenk*
I'm looking for something (a bit)...	Ich suche etwas (ein bisschen)... *ish zookher etvas (I-n biss-shen)*
...cheaper	...Billigeres *billigeres*
...better	...Besseres *besseres*
...darker	...Dunkleres *doonkleres*
...lighter (colour)	...Helleres *helleres*
...larger	...Größeres *grursseres*
...smaller	...Kleineres *klyneres*
I may come back later	Ich komme vielleicht später zurück *ish kommer feelysht shpaiter tsoorewk*
I (don't) like it	Es gefällt mir (nicht) *es gerfelt meer (nisht)*
May I try it/them on?	Darf ich es/sie anprobieren? *darf ish es/zee anprobeeren?*
I'll take it/them	Ich nehme es/sie *ish naimer es/zee*
I prefer that one	ich mag diesen lieber *ish maag deezen leeber*
Will you gift wrap it, please?	Können Sie es als Geschenk einpacken, bitte? *kurnen zee es als gershenk I-npaken, bitter?*
It's not what I'm looking for	Es ist nicht das, was ich suche *es ist nisht das, vas ish zookher*

PAYING

Where is the till/check out?	Wo ist die Kasse?
	voh ist dee kasser?
How much is it?	Wie viel kostet es?
	veefeel kostet es?
Do you take credit cards/ traveller's cheques?	Nehmen Sie Kreditkarten/ Reiseschecks?
	naimen zee kredeet-karten/ ryzer-sheks?
Is VAT included?	Ist Mehrwertsteuer inbegriffen?
	ist mairvairt-shtoyer inbergriffen?
Can you order it for me?	Können Sie es mir bitte bestellen?
	kurnen zee es meer bitter berstellen?
Can you send it to this address?	Können Sie es an diese Adresse schicken?
	kurnen zee es an deezer adresser schicken?
Can you deliver it?	Können Sie es liefern?
	kurnen zee es leefern?
How long will it take?	Wie lange dauert es?
	vee langer dowert es?
Could you wrap it as a present?	Können Sie es als Geschenk einpacken?
	kurnen zee ess als gershenk I-npacken?

You may hear:

Kann ich Ihnen helfen?	Can I help you?
kan ish eenen helfen?	
Werden Sie schon bedient?	Are you being served?
vairden zee shohn berdeent?	

Sonst noch etwas?
zonst nokh etvas?

Anything else?

Wie viel/wie viele möchten Sie?
veefeel/veefeeler murshten zee?

How much/how many would you like?

Möchten Sie es/sie anprobieren?
murshten zee es/zee anprobeeren?

Would you like to try it on?

Welche Farbe/Größe möchten Sie?
velsher faarber/grursser murshten zee?

What colour/size would you like?

PROBLEMS

I think you've made a mistake (on the bill)	Ich glaube, Sie haben sich verrechnet *ish glowber, zee haaben zish fair-reshnet*
I'd like to exchange this	Ich möchte das umtauschen *ish murshter das oomtowshen*
It's...	Es ist... *es ist...*
...the wrong size	...die falsche Größe *dee falsher grursser*
...faulty	...defekt *defekt*
I'd like a refund	Ich möchte mein Geld zurück-bekommen *ish murshter myn gelt tsoorewk-berkommen*
Here's the receipt	Hier ist die Quittung *heer ist dee kvitoong*
I bought it yesterday	Ich habe es gestern gekauft *ish haaber es gestern gerkowft*
It was a present	Es war ein Geschenk *es war I-n gershenk*

Where can I get this repaired?	Wo kann ich das reparieren lassen?
	voh kann ish das repareeren lassen?
When will it/will they be ready?	Wann ist es/sind sie fertig?
	van ist es/zint zee fairtig?

You may see:

Abteilung	department
Ausgang	exit
Ausverkauf	sale
ausverkauft	sold out
Campingzubehör	camping equipment
Eingang	entrance
Heimwerkerbedarf	DIY
Lebensmittel	groceries
Mode	fashion
nicht berühren	do not touch
Obergeschoss	upper floor
Preis	price
preiswert	good value
reduziert	reduced
Schreibwaren	stationery
Selbstbedienung	self-service
Sommerschlussverkauf	summer sale
Sonderangebot	special offer
Sonderpreis	special price
Spielwaren	toys
Süßwaren	sweets
Umtausch nur gegen Quittung	goods exchanged only with receipt

vergriffen	out of stock
Winterschlussverkauf	winter sale
Zeitungen/Zeitschriften	newspapers/magazines

SHOPS

Where's the...? | Wo ist...? |
| | *voh ist...?* |

...baker's	...die Bäckerei	*dee beker-I*
...bank	...die Bank	*dee bank*
...bookshop	...die Buchhandlung	*dee bookh-handloong*
...butcher's	...die Metzgerei	*dee metsger-I*
...cake-shop	...die Konditorei	*dee konditohr-I*
...camera shop	...das Fotogeschäft	*das fohto-gersheft*
...chemist's	...die Apotheke	*dee apotaiker*
...chemist's (non-dispensing)	...die Drogerie	*dee drohgeree*
...department store	...das Kaufhaus	*das kowf-hows*
...dry cleaner's	...die chemische Reinigung	*dee kaimisher runigoong*
...greengrocer's	...die Gemüsehandlung	*dee germewser-handloong*
...grocer's	...das Lebensmittelgeschäft	*das laibensmittel-gersheft*
...hypermarket	...der Großmarkt	*dair grohss-markt*
...jeweller's	...der Juwelier	*dair Yooveleer*
...laundrette	...der Waschsalon	*dair vash-zalon*
...newsagent's	...der Zeitungshändler	*dair tsytoongs-hendler*
...optician	...der Optiker	*dair optiker*
...post office	...das Postamt	*das posstamt*
...supermarket	...der Supermarkt	*dair zoopermarket*
...toy shop	...das Spielwarengeschäft	*das shpeelvaaren-gersheft*
...travel agent	...das Reisebüro	*das ryzer-bewroh*

AT A DEPARTMENT STORE

Where are the...?	Wo sind die...? *voh zint dee...?*
...CDs	...CDs *sai-daiz*
...sports goods	...Sportartikel *shport-artikel*
...books	...Bücher *bewsher*
Which floor?	In welchem Stock? *in velshem shtok?*
On the ground floor	Im Erdgeschoss *im airdgershoss*
In the basement	Im Untergeschoss *im oontergershoss*
On the first/second floor	Im ersten/zweiten Stock *im airsten/tsvyten shtok*
Toiletries	Toilettenartikel *twaletten-artikel*
Clothing and Shoes	Kleider und Schuhe *klyder oont shooer*
Electrical Goods	Elektrowaren *elektrovaaren*
Food	Lebensmittel *laibenzmittel*
Photographic Equipment	Fotoartikel *fohto-artikel*
Repairs	Reparaturen *reparatooren*

CLOTHES AND SHOES

I'd like something...
Ich möchte etwas...
ish murshter etvas...

...for me/her/him
...für mich/sie/ihn
fewr mish/zee/een

...to match this
...was dazu passt
vas datsoo passt

I take size...
Ich habe Größe...
ish haaber grursser...

(Where) can I try it on?
(Wo) kann ich es anprobieren?
(voh) kan ish es anprobeeren?

Is there a mirror?
Gibt es einen Spiegel?
gipt es I-nen shpeegel?

It doesn't fit
Es sitzt nicht sehr gut
es zitst nisht zair goot

It's too...
Es ist zu...
es ist tsoo...

...long/short
...lang/kurz
lang/koorts

...tight/loose
...eng/weit
eng/vyt

...big/small
...groß/klein
grohs/klyn

Can you alter it?
Können sie es ändern?
kurnen zee es endern?

I don't like the style/colour
Der Stil/die Farbe gefällt mir nicht
dair shteel/dee faarber gerfelt meer nisht

Do you have this in green?
Haben Sie das in grün?
haaben zee das in grewn?

Does it have to be handwashed?	Muss man das mit der Hand waschen?
	moos man das mit dair hant vashen?

You may hear:

Welche Größe haben Sie?	What size do you take?
velsher grurser haaben zee?	
Wir haben es nicht in dieser Farbe/Ihrer Größe	We don't have it in that colour/your size
veer haaben es nisht in deezer faarber/eerer grurser	
Der Spiegel/die Umkleidekabine ist da drüben	The mirror/fitting room is over there
dair shpeegel/dee oomklyderkabeener ist da drewben	

COLOURS AND FABRICS

black	schwarz	blue	blau
	shvarts		*bl-ow*
brown	braun	green	grün
	brown		*grewn*
orange	orange	yellow	gelb
	oronzher		*gelp*
red	rot	white	weiß
	roht		*vys*
light (grey)	hell (grau)	dark (pink)	dunkel (rosa)
	hell (grow)		*doonkel (rohza)*
cotton	Baumwolle	wool	Wolle
	bowmvoller		*voller*
leather	Leder	silk	Seide
	laider		*zyder*
suede	Wildleder	synthetic	synthetisch
	viltlaider		*zewntaitish*

SHOES

I'd like a pair of...	Ich möchte ein Paar... *ish murshter I-n paar...*
...shoes	...Schuhe *shoo-er*
...boots	...Stiefel *shteefel*
...trainers	...Turnschuhe *toorn-shooer*
...walking boots	...Wanderschuhe *vander-shooer*
Do you have a larger/ smaller pair?	Haben Sie ein größeres/ kleineres Paar? *haaben zee I-n grurseres/ klyneres paar?*
Do you have any...?	Haben Sie...? *haaben zee...?*
...insoles	...Einlegesohlen *I-nlaiger-zohlen*
...laces	...Schnürsenkel *shnewr-zenkel*
...polish	...Schuhcreme *shoo-kraimer*
Can I try them on?	Kann ich sie anprobieren? *kan ish zee anprobeeren?*
They're a bit uncomfortable	Sie sind ein bisschen unbequem *zee zint I-n biss-shen oon-berkvaim*

AT THE HAIRDRESSER'S/BARBER'S

Can you recommend a hairdresser?	Können Sie einen Friseur empfehlen? *kurnen zee I-nen frizur empfailen?*

Hairdressers in Germany are normally closed on Mondays.

I'd like an appointment for...	Ich möchte einen Termin am... *ish murshter I-nen tairmeen am...*
Just a trim, please	Nur etwas nachschneiden, bitte *noor etvas nakh-shnyden, bitter*
A cut and blow-dry	Schneiden und föhnen, bitte *shnyden oont furnen, bitter*
Not too short/long	Nicht zu kurz/lang *nisht tsoo koorts/lang*
A bit more off here	Hier etwas kürzer, bitte *heer etvas kewrtser, bitter*
Would you trim my beard/moustache?	Können Sie mir bitte den Bart/den Schnurrbart stutzen? *kurnen zee meer bitter dain bart/dain shnoorbart shtootsen?*
I'd like...	Ich möchte... *ish murshter...*
...the same style again	...nochmal den gleichen Schnitt *nokhmal dain glyshen shnit*
...highlights	...Strähnchen *shtrainshen*
...conditioner	...eine Haarspülung *I-ne haar-spewloong*

PHOTOGRAPHIC

I'd like a film/two films for this camera	Ich möchte einen Film/ zwei Filme für diesen Fotoapparat *ish murshter I-nen film/tsvy filmer fewr deezen fohto-aparaat*
black and white film	Schwarzweißfilm *shvaarts-vys-film*
colour film	Farbnegativfilm *faarbnegateef-film*
colour slide film	Farbdiafilm *faarb-deeafilm*
24/36 exposures	24/36 Aufnahmen *feer-oont-tsvantsig/zekhs-oont-drysig owfnaamen*
I'd like some passport photos taken	Ich möchte Passbilder machen lassen *ish murshter pasbilder makhen lassen*
Is processing included?	Ist der Preis mit Entwicklung? *ist dair prys mit entvikloong?*
How much is processing?	Was kostet die Entwicklung? *vas kostet dee entvikloong?*
How long will it take?	Wie lange dauert es? *vee langer dowert es?*
I'd like...copies/enlargements	Ich möchte...Abzüge/ Vergrößerungen *ish murshter...aptsewger/ fairgrurseroongen*
Can you repair my camera?	Können Sie meinen Fotoapparat reparieren? *kurnen zee mynen fohto-aparaat parareeren?*

Do you have any batteries?

Haben Sie Batterien?
haaben zee bateree-en?

AT THE CHEMIST'S

Where's the nearest
(all-night) chemist's?

Wo ist die nächste Apotheke
(mit Nachtdienst)?
*voh ist dee neshster apotaiker
(mit nakhtdeenst)?*

I want something for...

Ich möchte etwas gegen...
ish murshter etvas gaigen...

...diarrhoea

...Durchfall
doorshfal

...a headache

...Kopfschmerzen
kopfshmairtsen

...insect-bites

...Insektenstiche
inzektenshtisher

...a sore throat

...Halsschmerzen
hals-shmairtsen

...sunburn

...Sonnenbrand
zonnenbrant

...an upset stomach

...Magenverstimmung
maagen-fairshtimoong

Do I need a prescription for it?

Brauche ich ein Rezept dafür?
browkher ish I-n retsept dafewr?

It's for an adult/a child

Es ist für einen Erwachsenen/
ein Kind
*es ist fewr I-nen airvakhsenen/
I-n kint*

There are two types of chemist's in Germany:
The *Apotheke* is a pharmacist's. It can make up prescriptions
and sell drugs but it does not sell toiletries, films etc. When
closed, the address of the nearest chemist's which is open is
displayed in the window. At night ring the doorbell for service.
The *Drogerie* sells toiletries, non-prescription drugs etc. N.B. *Gift*
means 'poison'.

GROCERIES

• For items of food and drink, see the section beginning page 73.

Can I help myself?	Kann ich mich selbst bedienen? *kan ish mish zelbst berd<u>ee</u>nen?*
May I have a plastic bag?	Kann ich eine Plastiktüte haben? *kan ish <u>I</u>-ner pl<u>a</u>stik-tewter h<u>aa</u>ben?*
one/some of those	eins/einige von denen *I-ns/<u>I</u>-niger von d<u>ai</u>nen*
a piece/two pieces of...	ein Stück/zwei Stück... *I-n shtewk/tsvy shtewk...*
a slice/two slices of...	eine Scheibe/zwei Scheiben... *<u>I</u>-ner sh<u>y</u>ber/tsvy sh<u>y</u>ben...*
a bottle of...	eine Flasche... *<u>I</u>-ner fl<u>a</u>sher...*
a can/tin of...	eine Dose... *<u>I</u>-ner d<u>oh</u>zer...*
a jar of...	ein Glas... *I-n glaas...*
a packet of...	eine Packung/eine Tüte... *<u>I</u>-ner p<u>a</u>kkoong/<u>I</u>-ner t<u>ew</u>ter...*
a kilo of...	ein Kilo... *I-n k<u>ee</u>lo...*
a pound of...	ein Pfund... *I-n pfoont*
half a pound of...	ein halbes Pfund... *I-n h<u>a</u>lbes pfoont...*
200 grams of...	200 Gramm... *tsvy h<u>oo</u>ndert gram...*
a litre of...	ein Liter... *I-n l<u>ee</u>ter...*

MISCELLANEOUS

I'm looking for a present for...	Ich suche ein Geschenk für... *ish sookher I-n gershenk fewr...*
Do you have anything in gold/silver?	Haben Sie etwas in Gold/Silber? *haaben zie etvas in golt/zilber?*
Is that real silver?	Ist das Echtsilber? *ist das esht-zilber?*
I want a small present	Ich möchte ein kleines Geschenk *ish murshter I-n klyn-es gershenk*
I'd like a toy/game	Ich möchte ein Spielzeug/Spiel *ish murshter I-n shpeel-tsoyg/ shpeel*
Do you have any CDs by...?	Haben Sie CDs von...? *haaben zee sai-daiz fon...?*
I'd like a souvenir	Ich möchte ein Andenken *ish murshter I-n andenken*
It's for...	Es ist für... *es ist fewr...*
...my girlfriend/boyfriend	...meine Freundin/meinen Freund *myner froyndin/mynen froynt*
...my wife/ husband	...meine Frau/meinen Mann *myner frow/mynen man*
...my parents	...meine Eltern *myner eltern*

RELIGIOUS SERVICES AND CHURCHES

Where is...?	Wo ist...? *voh ist...?*
...the Catholic church	...die katholische Kirche *dee katohlisher keersher*
...the Protestant church	...die evangelische Kirche *dee evangailisher keersher*

...synagogue | ...die Synagoge
dee zewnagohger

At what time is...? | Wann beginnt...?
van bergint...?

...the mass | ...die Messe
dee messer

...the service | ...der Gottesdienst
dair gottesdeenst

Is there a...who speaks English? | Gibt es einen..., der Englisch spricht?
gipt es I-nen ..., dair ennglish shprisht?

...minister... | ...Pfarrer...
pfarrer...

...priest... | ...Priester...
preester...

...rabbi... | ...Rabbiner..
rabeener...

REPAIRS

Can you repair this? | Können Sie das reparieren?
kurnen zee das reparegeren?

There's something wrong with this | Etwas stimmt nicht damit
etvas shtimt nisht daamit

It works sometimes | Es funktioniert manchmal
es foonktsioneert manshmaal

It doesn't work | Es funktioniert nicht
es foonktsioneert nisht

It's jammed | Es klemmt
es klemt

It's broken | Es ist kaputt
es ist kapoot

It is usually possible to go into most churches, cathedrals etc. except when a service is in progress. In many larger towns you will find some services conducted in English. Ask at the local tourist office for details.

I can't close/open it

Ich kann es nicht zumachen/
aufmachen
*ish kan es nisht tsoomakhen/
owfmakhen*

How much will it cost?

Wie viel kostet es?
veefeel kostet es?

How long will it take?

Wie lange dauert es?
vee langer dowert es?

I'm here for two more
days/weeks

Ich bin noch 2 Tage/
Wochen hier
*ish bin nokh tsvy taager/
vokhen heer*

Is it worth it?

Lohnt es sich?
lohnt es zish?

You may hear:

Es lohnt sich nicht
es lohnt sish nisht

It's not worth it

Das lässt sich nicht reparieren
das lesst zish nisht repareeren

It can't be repaired

Dieses Modell wird nicht
mehr hergestellt
*deezes model virt nisht
mair hairgershtelt*

This model isn't produced
any more

Wir müssen die Ersatzteile
bestellen
*veer mewssen dee airzatstyler
bershtellen*

We'll have to order the parts

Es ist in 2 Tagen fertig
es ist in tsvy taagen fairtig

It'll be ready in 2 days

Wir müssen es wegschicken
veer mewssen es vaig-shiken

We'll have to send it away

Am besten lassen Sie es zu
Hause reparieren
*am besten lassen zee es tsoo
howzer repareeren*

It would be better to have it
repaired at home

SHOES

Where can I get my shoes
mended?

Wo kann ich diese Schuhe
reparieren lassen?
*voh kan ish deezer shoo-er
repareeren lassen?*

Can you repair these shoes?

Können Sie diese Schuhe
reparieren?
*kurnen zee deezer shoo-er
repareeren?*

Can you stitch this?

Können Sie das nähen?
kurnen zee das nai-en?

I want new soles/heels

Ich möchte neue Sohlen/Absätze
ish murshter noyer sohlen/apsetser

When will they be ready?

Wann sind sie fertig?
van zint zee fairtig?

BANKS AND POST OFFICES

• Credit cards are widely used for payment in shops, restaurants and
hotels.

• When changing money in banks, it is normal to fill in the forms at
one counter, but to collect the money from another.

• Banking hours: 8.30-12.30 and 13.30-16.00 (18.00 on
Thursdays). Outside these hours look for currency exchange shops
(*Geldwechsel* or *Wechselstube*).

• Germany/Austria: 1 Euro = 100 cent

  Switzerland: I Fr (Franken) = 100 Rp (Rappen)

BANK

Where is the nearest bank?	Wo ist die nächste Bank/ Sparkasse? *voh ist dee neshster bank/ shpaarkasser?*
I'd like to change some pounds/dollars into Euros	Ich möchte Pfund/Dollar in Euro wechseln *ish murshter pfoont/dollaar in oyroh vekhseln*
I'd like to cash a traveller's cheque/ Eurocheque	Ich möchte einen Reisescheck/ Euroscheck einlösen *ish murshter I-nen ryzershek/oyroshek I-nlurzen*
I'd like to buy some Euros with my credit card	Ich möchte Euros mit meiner Kreditkarte kaufen *ish murshter oyrohs mit myner kredeetkaarter kowfen*
What's the exchange rate for the pound?	Wie ist der Kurs für das Pfund? *vee ist dair koorz fewr das pfoont?*
Here is my passport	Hier ist mein Pass *heer ist myn pass*
I'd like notes/some small change	Ich möchte Scheine/etwas Kleingeld *ish murshter shyner/etvas klyngelt*
Where should I sign?	Wo muss ich unterschreiben? *voh moos ish oonter-shryben?*
I'd like to deposit this money	Ich möchte dieses Geld einzahlen *ish murshter deezes Geld I-n-tsaalen*
I'd like to transfer some money	Ich möchte Geld überweisen *ish murshter gelt ewbervysen*
I'd like to withdraw some money	Ich möchte Geld abheben *ish murshter gelt abhaiben*

I'd like to open an account	Ich möchte ein Konto eröffnen *ish murshter I-n konto air-urfnen*
Where should I sign?	Wo muss ich unterschreiben? *voh moos ish oonter-shryben?*
I want to pay this into my account	Ich möchte das auf mein Konto einzahlen *ish murshter das owf myn konto I-n-tsaalen*

You may hear:

Wie viel möchten Sie wechseln? *veefeel murshten zee vekhlseln?*	How much would you like to change?
Kann ich Ihren Pass sehen? *kan ish eeren pass zai-en?*	May I see your passport?
Ohne Pass können wir Reiseschecks nicht einlösen *ohner pass kurnen veer ryzersheks nicht I-nlurzen*	We can't change traveller's cheques without a passport
Bitte füllen Sie dieses Formular aus *bitter fewlen zee deezes formoolaar ows*	Please fill in this form
Bitte unterschreiben Sie hier *bitter oontershryben zee heer*	Please sign here
Nehmen Sie dieses Papier/diese Nummer *naimen zee deezes papeer/deezer noomer*	Take this piece of paper/this number
Gehen Sie an Kasse Nummer... *gai-en zee an kasser noomer...*	Go to counter number...
Wie darf ich Ihnen das Geld geben? *vee daarf ish eenen das gelt gaiben?*	How would you like the money?
Das ist Ihre Quittung *das ist eerer kvittong*	Here's your receipt

Das macht…	That comes to…
das makht…	
Gehen Sie an Schalter (4)	Go to counter (4)
gai-en zee an shallter (feer)	

You may see:

Bank	Bank
Devisen	Foreign currency
Geldautomat	Cash dispenser
Geldwechsel	Currency exchange
Kasse	Cash desk
Schalterstunden } Schalterzeiten	Opening hours
Sorten	Foreign currency
Sparkasse	Savings bank
Wechselstube	Currency exchange

N.B. *Spielbank* is a casino.

POST OFFICE

Opening times:-

> **Germany**
> 8.00-18.00; Saturday 8.00-13.00
>
> **Austria**
> 8.00-12.00, 14.00-17.00; Saturday 8.00-11.00
>
> **Switzerland**
> 7.30-12.00, 13.30-18.30; Saturday 8.00-11.00

Where is the nearest post office/letterbox?	Wo ist das nächste Postamt/der nächste Briefkasten? *voh ist das neshster posstamt/dair neshster breefkasten?*

An 80-cent stamp, please	Eine Briefmarke zu 80 cent, bitte *I-ner breefmarker tsoo akhtsig sent, bitter*
5 1-Euro stamps, please	Fünf Briefmarken zu 1 Euro, bitte *fewnf breefmaarken tsoo I-nem oyroh bitter*
What's the cost of...?	Was kostet...? *vas kostet...?*
...a letter to America?	...ein Brief nach Amerika *I-n breef nakh amerika*
...a postcard to England	...eine Postkarte nach England *I-ner postkaarter nakh englant*
...this parcel	...dieses Paket *deezes pakait*
Can you weigh this letter/ this parcel?	Können Sie bitte diesen Brief/dieses Paket wiegen? *kurnen zee bitter deezen breef/deezes pakait veegen?*
I'd like to send it...	Ich möchte es...schicken *ish murshter es...shicken*
...by air mail...	...per Luftpost... *pair looftposst...*
...express delivery...	...per Eilpost... *pair I-lposst...*
...letter post...	...als Brief... *als breef...*
...parcel post...	...als Paket... *als pakait...*
...surface mail...	...per Normaltarif... *pair normaaltareef...*

Post offices are recognisable by the word *Post(amt)* and the symbol of the post horn. Letter boxes are yellow.

...registered delivery...

...per Einschreiben...
pair I-nshryben...

Is there any post for me?

Ist Post für mich da?
ist posst fewr mish daa?

You may see:

Ausland	Foreign (counter)
ausländische Währungen	foreign currency
Auszahlungen	withdrawals
Brief(e)	letter(s)
Briefkasten	Letter box
Briefmarkenautomat	Stamp dispenser
Bundespost	Federal Post Office
Fernsprecher	Telephone
Geldwechsel	currency exchange
Nächste Leerung	Next collection
Päckchen	small parcels
Pakete	Parcels
Post(amt)	post office
Postkarte(n)	post card(s)
Postlagernde Sendungen	Post restante
Postleitzahl	post code
Postwertzeichen	Stamps
Sondermarken	Commemorative stamps

COMMUNICATIONS

TELEPHONE

• Most telephone boxes have instructions in English and German as well as diagrams. International calls can also be made from most of them, or you can go to the counter marked *Ferngespräche* in larger post offices, where you will be allocated a telephone booth. You pay after you have finished your call.

• When making phone calls abroad, remember to omit the first 0 of the area code following the country code: e.g. when phoning Cambridge from Germany, dial 0044 (England), then 1223 (not 01223), followed by the number.

Where's...?	Wo ist...? *voh ist...?*
...the telephone	...das Telefon *das telefohn*
...the nearest telephone box	...die nächste Telefonzelle *dee neshster telefohn-tseller*
May I use the phone?	Darf ich das Telefon benutzen? *daarf ish das telefohn bernootsen?*
Hallo, this is...	Hallo, hier... *hallo, heer...*
May I speak to...?	Kann ich...sprechen, bitte? *kan ish...sphreshen bitter?*
May I have extension number...?	Ich möchte Apparat... *ish murshter aparaat...*
I'll phone again later	Ich rufe wieder an *ish roofer veeder an*

On the phone, 2 is pronounced *tsvoh*, to avoid confusion with 3 (*dry*).

When can I get him/her?

Wann kann ich ihn/sie erreichen?
van kan ish een/zee airryshen?

Can I leave a message?

Können Sie etwas ausrichten?
kurnen zee etvas owsrishten?

My name is...

Ich heiße...
ish hysser...

Please tell him/her I called

Bitte sagen Sie ihm/ihr, dass ich
angerufen habe
*bitter zaagen zee eem/eer, das ish
angeroofen haaber*

Could you ask him/her
to phone me?

Können Sie ihn/sie bitten,
mich anzurufen?
*kurnen zee een/zee bitten, mish
antsooroofen?*

between 5 and 7 o'clock

zwischen 5 und 7 Uhr
tsvishen fewnf oont zeeben oor

My phone number is...

Meine Telefonnummer ist...
myner telefohn-noomer ist...

OPERATOR

What's the code for...

Was ist die Vorwahl für...?
vas ist dee fohrvaal fewr...?

I'd like to make a call to America

Ich möchte nach Amerika anrufen
*ish murshter nakh amerika
anroofen*

What's the number for
(international) directory
enquiries?

Welche Nummer hat die
(internationale) Auskunft?
*velsher noomer hat dee
(internatsionaaler) owskoonft?*

What's the number for the
(international) operator?

Welche Nummer hat die
(internationale) Vermittlung?
*velsher noomer hat dee
(internatsionaaler) fairmitloong?*

Could you help me to get this number?	Können Sie mir helfen, diese Nummer zu bekommen? *kurnen zee meer helfen, deezer noomer tsoo berkommen?*
I can't get through	Ich komme nicht durch *ish kommer nisht doorsh*
I want to make a reverse charge call	Ich möchte ein R-Gespräch *ish murshter I-n air-gershpraish*
I've been cut off	Ich bin unterbrochen worden *ish bin oonterbrokhen vorden*
I dialled the wrong number	Ich habe mich verwählt *ish haaber mish fairvailt*
I was given the wrong number	Man hat mich falsch verbunden *man hat mish falsh verboonden*
What did the call cost?	Was hat das Gespräch gekostet? *vas hat das gershpraish gerkostet?*

ELECTRONIC

I'd like to send a fax	Ich möchte ein Fax schicken *ish murshter I-n fax shicken*
Can I send a fax/e-mail from here?	Kann ich von hier faxen/mailen? *kan ish fon heer faxen/mailen?*
What's your e-mail address/ fax number?	Wie ist Ihre E-Mail-Adresse/ Faxnummer? *vee ist eerer 'E' mail-adresser/ faxnoomer?*
Can you text me?	Können Sie mir simsen/texten? *kurnen zee meer zimzen/texten?*
What's your mobile number?	Wie ist Ihre Handy-Nummer? *vee ist eerer handi-noomer?*

You may see:

Auskunft	Enquiries
außer Betrieb	out of order

Auslandsgespräche	Foreign calls
bitte zahlen	Please insert more money
Ferngespräch/Ferngespräche	long-distance call(s)
Feuerwehr	fire brigade
Gelbe Seiten	Yellow Pages
Geldeinwurf/Geld einwerfen	insert coins
Gespräch	call
Großbritannien	Great Britain
Hörer abnehmen	lift the receiver
Krankenhaus	hospital
Inlandsgespräche	Phone calls within the country
Münzfreier Notruf	Free emergency services calls
Münzeinwurf	Insert coins
Münzrückgabe	Returned coins
Notruf	emergency phone
Ortsgespräch(e)	local call(s)
Polizei	police
Telefonkarte	phone card
Vorwahl	dialling code
wählen	to dial
Webseite(n)	website(s)

The Alphabet

a aa	**g** gai	**m** emm	**s** ess	**y** ewpsilon
b bai	**h** haa	**n** enn	**t** tai	**z** tsett
c tsai	**i** ee	**o** oh	**u** uh	**ß** ess-tsett
d dai	**j** yot	**p** pai	**v** fow	(=ss)
e ai	**k** kaa	**q** kuh	**w** vai	
f eff	**l** ell	**r** air	**x** ix	

The accent ¨ is called the **umlaut** (*oomlowt*):

ä *aa oomlowt/ ai*   ö *oh oomlowt/ ur*   ü *uh oomlowt/ ew*

How do you spell that?	Wie schreibt man das? *vee shrypt man das?*
It's spelt …	Das schreibt man … *das shrypt man …*

You may hear:

Wer ist am Apparat? *vair ist am apparaat?*	Who's speaking?
Einen Moment, bitte *I-nen moment bitter*	Just a minute; hold on, please
Bleiben Sie dran *blyben zee dran*	Hold the line
Er/sie ist zur Zeit nicht da *er/zee ist tsoor tsyt nisht daa*	He/she isn't in at the moment
Es ist besetzt *es ist berzetst*	The line's engaged
Es antwortet niemand *es antvortet neemant*	There's no answer
Können Sie später wieder anrufen? *kurnen zee shpaiter veeder anroofen?*	Could you phone back later?
Kann er/sie Sie zurückrufen? *kan er/zee zee tsoorewk-roofen?*	Can he/she phone you back?
Kann ich ihm/ihr etwas ausrichten? *kan ish eem/eer etvas owsrishten?*	Can I give him/her a message?
Sind Sie telefonisch zu erreichen? *zint zee telefohnish tsoo erryshen?*	Can you be reached by phone?

Sie haben sich verwählt
zee haaben zish fairvailt

You've got the wrong number

Welche Nummer haben
Sie gewählt?
*velsher noomer haaben
zee gervailt?*

What number did you dial?

ESSENTIAL INFORMATION

ACCIDENT

For emergency numbers, see page 154.

Help!	Hilfe!
	hilfer!
Stop!	Halt!
	halt!
Please send an ambulance	Bitte schicken Sie einen Krankenwagen
	bitter schicken zee I-nen kranken-waagen
There's been an accident	Es ist ein Unfall passiert
	es ist I-n oonfal paseert

on the road from...to...	auf der Straße zwischen...und... *owf dair shtraasser tsvishen...oont...*
about 4km from...	ungefähr vier Kilometer von... *oon-gefair feer kilomaiter fon...*
Where's the nearest phone?	Wo ist das nächste Telefon? *vo ist das nekhster telefohn?*
Please call the police	Rufen Sie bitte die Polizei *roofen zee bitter dee polits-I*
Call a doctor quickly	Rufen Sie schnell einen Arzt *roofen zee shnell I-nen aartst*
There are people injured	Es hat Verletzte gegeben *es hat fairletster gergaiben*
Police	Polizei *polits-I*
Ambulance	Krankenwagen *kranken-vaagen*
My/your registration number	meine/Ihre Autonummer *myner/eerer owtoh-noomer*
My/your name	mein/Ihr Name *myn/eer naamer*
my/your address	meine/Ihre Adresse *myner/eerer adresser*
My/your driving licence	mein/Ihr Führerschein *myn/eer fewrer-shyn*
My/your insurance company	Meine/Ihre Versicherungsgesellschaft *myner/eerer fairzisheroongs-gerselshaft*

THEFT AND LOST PROPERTY

Where is...?	Wo ist...? *voh ist.../*
...the lost property office	...das Fundbüro *das foontbewroh*
...the police station	...das Polizeirevier *das polits-I-reveer*
I'd like to report...	Ich möchte...melden *ish murshter...melden*
...a loss...	...einen Verlust... *I-nen fairloost...*
...a theft...	...einen Diebstahl... *I-nen deepshtaal...*
I've been mugged	Ich bin überfallen worden *ish bin ewberfallen wohrden*
My...has been stolen	Mein/meine...ist gestohlen worden *myn/myner...ist gerstohlen vorden*
I've lost...	Ich habe...verloren *ish haaber...fairlohren*
...my car...	... mein Auto... *myn owtoh...*
...my handbag...	... meine Handtasche... *myner hant-tasher...*
...my luggage...	... mein Gepäck... *myn gerpeck...*
...my camera...	...meinen Fotoapparat... *mynen fohto-aparaat...*
...my cheque book...	...mein Scheckheft... *myn shek-heft...*

Look for the sign *Fundamt*, *Fundbüro* or *Fundsachen*. In smaller towns, this is often the town hall. In case of thefts, go to the police station.

...my credit card...	...meine Kreditkarte...
	myner kredeetkaarter...
...money...	...Geld...
	gelt...
...my traveller's cheques...	...meine Reiseschecks...
	myner ryzersheks...
...my umbrella...	...meinen Regenschirm...
	mynen raigensheerm...
...my wallet...	...meine Brieftasche...
	myner breeftasher...
It's made of...	Es ist aus...
	es ist ows...
...cloth	...Stoff
	shtoff
...cotton	...Baumwolle
	bowmvoller
...gold	...Gold
	golt
...leather	...Leder
	laider

• For colours and fabrics, see page 128.

It's worth about...	Es ist ungefähr...wert
	es ist oon-gefair...vairt
It has my name...	Es hat meinen Namen...
	es hat mynen naamen...
...on it	...darauf
	daarowf
...inside	...darin
	daarin
I lost it at the station	Ich habe es auf dem Bahnhof verloren
	ish haaber es owf daim baanhohf fairloren

...at about 3 o'clock	...gegen 3 Uhr *gaigen dry oor*
...today	...heute *hoyter*
...yesterday	...gestern *gestern*
I don't know when/where I lost it	Ich weiß nicht, wo/wann ich es verloren habe *ish vys nisht, voh/van ish es fairloren haaber*
My room has been broken into	In mein Zimmer ist eingebrochen worden *in myn tsimmer ist I-ngerbrochen wohrden*
My car's been broken into	Mein Auto ist aufgebrochen worden *myn owtoh ist owfgerbrochen wohrden*
I've locked myself out	Ich habe mich ausgesperrt *ish haaber mish owsgeshpairt*
My son/my daughter has disappeared	Mein Sohn/meine Tochter ist verschwunden *myn zohn/myner tokhter ist fairshvoonden*

You may hear

Wo sind Sie?
voh sint zee?

Where are you?

Können Sie ihn/sie/es
beschreiben?
kurnen zee ihn bershryben?

Can you describe him/her/it?

Wo/Wie ist das passiert?
voh/vee ist das passeert?

Where/how did it happen?

Bleiben Sie am Apparat
blyben zee am apparaat

Please hold the line

Bitte füllen Sie dieses
Formular aus
*bitter fewlen zee deezes
formoolaar ows*

Please fill in this form

You may see:

Bergwacht	Mountain rescue
Erste Hilfe	First aid
Feuer	Fire
Feuerlöscher	Fire extinguisher
Fundbüro	Lost property office
Krankenhaus/Klinik	hospital
Lebensgefahr	(mortal) danger
Nachtdienst	late-night chemist
Notausgang	emergency exit
Notfallstation	Accident and emergency unit
Notruf	emergency phone call
Notrufsäule	emergency telephone
Polizei	police

EMERGENCY TELEPHONE

	Austria	Germany	Switzerland
Ambulance	144	112	117
Fire	122	112	118
Police	133	110	117

CLOTHING SIZES

Waist/Chest measurements

Inches	28	30	32	34	36	38	40	42	44	46
cms	71	76	80	87	91	97	102	107	112	117

Women

Dresses

European	36	38	40	42	44	46
British	10	12	14	16	18	20
US	8	10	12	14	16	18

Shoes

European	36	37	38	39	40	41
British	4	4½	5	5½	6	6½
US	6	6½	7	7½	8	8½

Men

Jackets/Coats

European	46	48	50	52	54	56
British/US	36	38	40	42	44	46

Shirts

European	36	37	38	39	41	42	43
British/US	14	14½	15	15½	16	16½	17

Shoes

European	38	39	41	42	43	44	45
British	5	6	7	8	8½ /9	9½ /10	11
US	6½	7	8	8½	9	9½	10

NUMBERS

0	null	*nul*	11	elf	*elf*
1	eins	*I-ns*	12	zwölf	*tsvurlf*
2	zwei	*tsvy*	13	dreizehn	*dr<u>y</u>tsain*
	zwo	*tsvoh (on the phone)*	14	vierzehn	*f<u>ee</u>rtsain*
3	drei	*dry*	15	fünfzehn	*f<u>ew</u>nftsain*
4	vier	*feer*	16	sechzehn	*z<u>e</u>khtsain*
5	fünf	*fewnf*	17	siebzehn	*z<u>ee</u>ptsain*
6	sechs	*zekhs*	18	achtzehn	*<u>a</u>khtsain*
7	sieben	*z<u>ee</u>ben*	19	neunzehn	*n<u>oy</u>ntsain*
8	acht	*akht*	20	zwanzig	*tsv<u>a</u>ntsig*
9	neun	*noyn*	21	einundzwanzig	*I-n-*
10	zehn	*tsain*			*oont-tsv<u>a</u>ntsig*

i.e 'one-and-twenty'. All 'tens and units' numbers work like this.

30	dreißig	*dr<u>y</u>sig*
40	vierzig	*f<u>ee</u>rtsig*
50	fünfzig	*f<u>ew</u>nftsig*
60	sechzig	*z<u>e</u>khtsig*
70	siebzig	*z<u>ee</u>ptsig*
80	achtzig	*<u>a</u>khtsig*
90	neunzig	*n<u>oy</u>ntsig*
100	hundert	*h<u>oo</u>ndert*
101	hunderteins	*hoondert-<u>y</u>ns*
200	zweihundert	*tsvy-h<u>oo</u>ndert*
1000	(ein)tausend	*(I-n) t<u>ow</u>zent*
1100	tausendeinhundert	*t<u>ow</u>zent-I-yn-h<u>oo</u>ndert*
2000	zweitausend	*tsvy-t<u>ow</u>zent*
1000000	eine Million	*I-ner mili<u>oh</u>n*

1st	erste *airster*	once	einmal *I-nmaal*
2nd	zweite *tsvyter*	twice	zweimal *tsvymaal*
3rd	dritte *dritter*	10th	zehnte *tsainter*
4th	vierte *feerter*	20th	zwanzigste *tsvantsigster*

MONTHS

January	Januar *yanooaar*	July	Juli *yooli*
February	Februar *febrooaar*	August	August *owgoost*
March	März *mairts*	September	September *zeptember*
April	April *apreel*	October	Oktober *oktohber*
May	Mai *my*	November	November *nohvember*
June	Juni *yooni*	December	Dezember *daitsember*

DAYS

Sunday	Sonntag *zontaag*	Thursday	Donnerstag *donnerztaag*
Monday	Montag *mohntaag*	Friday	Freitag *frytaag*
Tuesday	Dienstag *deenstaag*	Saturday	Samstag *zamstaag* Sonnabend (N. Germany) *zonaabent*
Wednesday	Mittwoch *mitvokh*		

DATES

in (the) summer	im Sommer *im zommer*
What's the date today?	Der Wievielte ist heute? *dair veefeelter ist hoyter?*
It's the 3rd August	Es ist der dritte August *es ist dair dritter owgoost*
(at the) beginning/end of June	Anfang/Ende Juni *anfang/ender yooni*
(in the) middle of May	Mitte Mai *mitter my*
by/until July	bis Juli *bis yooli*
in October	im Oktober *im oktohber*
since August	seit August *zyt owgoost*
last/next month	letzten/nächsten Monat *letsten/neshsten mohnaat*
on Tuesday	am Dienstag *am deenstaag*
last/next Friday	letzten/nächsten Freitag *letsten/neshsten frytaag*
on Thursdays	Donnerstags *donnerztagz*
on 19th July	am neunzehnten Juli *am noyntsainten yooli*
today/tomorrow/yesterday	heute/morgen/gestern *hoyter/morgen/gestern*
two days ago	vor zwei Tagen *for tsvy taagen*

in four days' time	in vier Tagen *in feer taagen*
at the weekend	am Wochenende *am vokhenender*

TIME

What time is it?	Wie viel Uhr ist es? *vee feel oor ist es?*
It's...	Es ist... *es ist...*
...1.00	...ein Uhr *I-n oor*
...1.05	...fünf nach eins *fewnf nakh I-ns*
...1.15	...viertel nach eins *feertel nakh I-ns*
...1.20	...zwanzig nach eins *tsvantsig nakh eins*
...1.30	...halb zwei *halp tsvy*
...1.50	....zehn vor zwei *tsain for tsvy*
...12.00 midday midnight	...zwölf Uhr Mittag Mitternacht *tsvurlf oor mittaag* *mitternakht*
in the morning/afternoon/ evening	morgens/nachmittags abends *morgerns/nakmitaagz/* *aabénts*

In German 'half past' is 'half to' the next hour.

PUBLIC HOLIDAYS

• National holidays are shown: there are local variations.

Austria = A	Germany = G		Switzerland = S
1 Jan	New Year's Day *Neujahr*	A G	S
6 Jan	Epiphany *Dreikönigstag*	A	
1 May	Labour Day *Tag der Arbeit*	A G	
17 June	German Unity Day *Tag der Deutschen Einheit*	G	
1 Aug	National Day *Nationalfeiertag*		S
15 Aug	Assumption *Mariä Himmelfahrt*	A	
26 Oct	National Day *Nationalfeiertag*	A	
1 Nov	All Saints' Day *Allerheiligen*	A	
8 Dec	Immaculate Conception *Mariä Empfängnis*	A	
25/6 Dec	Christmas *Weihnachten*	A G	S

DICTIONARY

Numbers, days, seasons are given on pages 156–157.

Food starts on page 88.

Where appropriate, feminine versions of nouns are given in brackets, e.g. student: (die) Student(in) = der Student (m)/die Studentin (f).

The polite versions are indicated by (P) and the familiar by (F).

A

a ein/eine

about (number) ungefähr

    (time) gegen

above über

to accept nehmen

accident der Unfall

accommodation die Unterkunft

account das Konto

it aches es tut weh

across über

AIDS AIDS

adaptor der Adapter

address die Adresse

admission der Eintritt

adult der/die Erwachsene

after nach

afternoon der Nachmittag

again nochmal

against gegen

...ago vor...

air conditioning die Klimaanlage

airline die Fluglinie

by airmail per Luftpost

airport der Flughafen

alarm clock der Wecker

all (of them) alle

allergic to allergisch gegen

alone allein

already schon

also auch

always immer

am: I am ich bin

ambulance der Krankenwagen

America Amerika

American (adj.) amerikanisch

and und

animal das Tier

ankle der Knöchel

another (different) ein anderer

another (more) noch ein

to answer antworten

antibiotic das Antibiotikum

antiseptic cream die Wundsalbe

any (pl) einige

any more noch mehr

any others andere

apartment die Wohnung

appointment die Termin, die Verabredung

are: we/they are wir/sie sind
you are Sie sind (P), du bist (F)
arm der Arm
arrival die Ankunft
to arrive ankommen
art die Kunst
art gallery die Kunstgalerie
as soon as possible so bald wie
                                              möglich
ashtray der Aschenbecher
to ask fragen
  to ask for bitten um
aspirin das Aspirin
asthma das Asthma
at (place) an
  (time) um
  (someone's) bei
aunt die Tante
Australia Australien
Austria Österreich
automatic automatisch

B

baby das Baby
baby food die Babynahrung
back (body) der Rücken
  (direction) zurück
    at the back hinten
bad schlecht
bag die Tasche
baker's die Bäckerei
balcony der Balkon
ball der Ball
bandage der Verband

bank die Bank
bank note der (Geld)/Schein
bar (drink) die Bar
bath das Bad
  to have a bath ein Bad
                                    nehmen
bathroom das Badezimmer
battery die Batterie
beach der Strand
beard der Bart
beautiful schön
bed das Bett
bed linen die Bettwäsche
beer das Bier
before vor
to begin beginnen
beginner der Anfänger
behind hinter
Belgium Belgien
below unter
belt der Gürtel
best beste
better besser
between zwischen
bicycle das Fahrrad
big groß
bill die Rechnung
birthday der Geburtstag
bite (insect) der Stich/der Biss
bitter bitter
black schwarz
blanket die Decke
to bleed bluten

blister   die Blase
blood   das Blut
blood pressure   der Blutdruck
blouse   die Bluse
blue   blau
boat   das Schiff, das Boot
body   der Körper
to boil   kochen
bone   der Knochen
bonnet (car)   die Motorhaube
book   das Buch
to book   reservieren
booking office   der Reservierungsschalter
boot (car)   der Kofferraum
   (shoe)   der Stiefel
born: I was b. in...   ich bin in ... geboren
border   die Grenze
boring   langweilig
to borrow   leihen
both   beide
bottle   die Flasche
bottle-opener   der Flaschenöffner
bottom (body)   der Hintern
bowl   die Schüssel
box   die Schachtel
box office   die Kasse
boy   der Junge
boyfriend   der Freund
bra   der Büstenhalter/BH
bracelet   das Armband

to brake   bremsen
brakes   die Bremse
brandy   der Weinbrand
bread   das Brot
to break   brechen
breakdown   die Panne
breakdown truck   der Abschleppwagen
breakfast   das Frühstück
breast   die Brust
to breathe   atmen
bridge   die Brücke
to bring   bringen
British (adj)   britisch
broken (bone)   gebrochen
   (machine)   kaputt
brother   der Bruder
brown   braun
bruise   die Quetschung
building   das Gebäude
burn (injury)   die Brandwunde
to burn   brennen
bus   der Bus
bus station   der Busbahnhof
business   das Geschäft
   on...   geschäftlich
busy (café)   voll
   (lots to do)   beschäftigt
but   aber
butane gas   das Butangas
butcher's   die Fleischerei/ Metzgerei
butter   die Butter

button   der Knopf
to buy   kaufen
by (author, maker)   von
   (time)   bis
   (next to)   neben

C

cable car   die Drahtseilbahn
café   das Café
cake   der Kuchen
calculator   der Rechner
call (summon)   rufen
   (phone)   anrufen
   (what's this called?)   Wie heißt das?
calm   ruhig
camera   der Fotoapparat
to camp   zelten
campsite   der Campingplatz
can (able to)   können
   (of food)   die Dose
canal   der Kanal
Canada   Kanada
to cancel   annullieren
candle   der Kerze
canoe   das Kanu
car   das Auto/der Wagen
car park   der Parkplatz
caravan   der Wohnwagen
carriage (rail)   der Wagen
cash   das Bargeld
cash desk   die Kasse
cash dispenser   der Geld-automat

to cash   einlösen
castle   das Schloss, die Burg
cathedral   der Dom, die Kathedrale
CD player   der CD-Spieler
cellar   der Keller
centre   die Mitte
chain   die Kette
chair   der Stuhl
Channel Tunnel   der Kanaltunnel
change (money)   das Kleingeld
to change
   (alter)   ändern
   (money)   wechseln
   (trains)   umsteigen
charge   die Gebühr/der Tarif
cheap   billig
to check   kontrollieren
   to check in   einchecken
   to check out   abreisen
checkout (shop)   die Kasse
checkup (medical)   die Untersuchung
cheers!   Prost!
cheese   der Käse
chemist   die Apotheke/ Drogerie
cheque   der Scheck
cheque book   das Scheckbuch
cheque card   die Scheckkarte
chest   die Brust
child   das Kind
chips   die Pommes frites
chocolate   die Schokolade

to choose wählen
Christian name der Vorname
church die Kirche
cider der Apfelwein
cigar die Zigarre
cigarette die Zigarette
cigarette lighter das Feuerzeug
cinema das Kino
circle (theatre) der Rang
city die Stadt
class die Klasse
clean sauber
to clean reinigen
clear klar
cling film die Lebensmittelfolie
cloakroom die Garderobe
clock die Uhr
to close schließen
closed geschlossen
cloth der Stoff
clothes die Kleider
cloud die Wolke
clutch (car) die Kupplung
coach der Bus
coat der Mantel
coathanger der Kleiderbügel
coffee der Kaffee
coin die Münze
cold (illness) die Erkältung
     (adj) kalt
colour die Farbe
comb der Kamm
to come kommen

comfortable bequem
Compact Disc die CD
compartment das Abteil
complicated kompliziert
concert das Konzert
concert hall die Konzerthalle
conditioner die Haarspülung
condom das Kondom
conference die Konferenz
conference centre
     die Kongresshalle
to confirm bestätigen
congratulations! herzlichen
     Glückwunsch!
connection (transport)
     der Anschluss
constipation die Verstopfung
contact lens die Kontaktlinse
to contain enthalten
contraceptive
     das Verhütungsmittel
contract der Vertrag
to cook kochen
corkscrew der Korkenzieher
to cost kosten
cot das Kinderbett
cotton die Baumwolle
cotton wool die Watte
cough der Husten
country das Land
cousin der (die) Cousin(e)
cramp der Krampf
cream (milk) die Sahne

credit card die Kreditkarte
crisps die Chips
to cross überqueren
cross-country skiing
                    der Langlauf
crossroads die Kreuzung
crowded voll, überfüllt
cup die Tasse
cupboard der Schrank
currency die Währung
current (electric, water)
                    der Strom
curtain der Vorhang
customs die Zollabfertigung
to cut schneiden
cut (wound) die Schnittwunde
cycling das Radfahren

D

damp feucht
to dance tanzen
dangerous gefährlich
dark dunkel
daughter die Tochter
day der Tag
dead tot
deaf taub
deckchair der Liegestuhl
deep tief
delay die Verspätung
to deliver liefern
Denmark Dänemark
dentist der Zahnarzt
denture die Zahnprothese

deodorant das Deodorant
department die Abteilung
department store das Kaufhaus
departure die Abfahrt,
                    der Abflug
to leave a deposit
        eine Sicherheit hinterlegen
dessert der Nachtisch
detour (road) die Umleitung
to develop entwickeln
diabetic der (die) Diabetiker(in)
dialling code die Vorwahl
diamond der Diamant
diarrhoea der Durchfall
dictionary das Wörterbuch
diesel das Diesel
different (other) andere
            (various) verschiedene
difficult schwierig
dining car der Speisewagen
dining room (hotel)
                    der Speisesaal
dinner (evening meal)
                    das Abendessen
direct direkt
to direct (to) den Weg zeigen
direction die Richtung
dirty schmutzig
disabled person
                    der/die Behinderte
to dislocate verrenken
dissatisfied unzufrieden
divorced geschieden
to do machen

doctor der Arzt
door die Tür
dormitory der Schlafraum
double room das Doppelzimmer
down hinunter
downhill skiing der Abfahrtslauf
downstairs unten
dress das Kleid
drink das Getränk
to drink trinken
drinking water das Trinkwasser
to drip (tap) tropfen
to drive fahren
driver der Fahrer
driving licence der Führerschein
drunk betrunken
dry trocken
dry cleaners
        die chemische Reinigung
duty-free zollfrei
duvet die Steppdecke

E

each jeder/jede/jedes
ear das Ohr
early früh
east der Osten/(adj) östlich
easy leicht
to eat essen
either of them es ist egal
either ... or ...
        entweder ... oder ...
electric(al) elektrisch
electricity der Stromanschluss

e-mail (address)
    der E-Mail (die E-Mail Adresse)
embarrassing peinlich
emergency der Notfall
empty leer
end das Ende
to end enden
engaged (couple) verlobt
        (in use) besetzt
engine (car) der Motor
England England
enlargement die Vergrößerung
English (adj) englisch
    I'm English ich bin Engländer
enough genug
entertainment die Unterhaltung
entrance der Eingang
entrance fee der Eintritt
envelope der Umschlag
equipment die Ausrüstung
escalator die Rolltreppe
especially besonders
Europe Europa
EU die Europäische Union
evening der Abend
evening meal das Abendessen
every/everyone jeder
everything alles
everywhere überall
exact(ly) genau
for example zum Beispiel
except (for) außer
to exchange (goods)
                umtauschen

exchange rate der Wechselkurs

excursion der Ausflug

exhaust pipe der Auspuff

exhibition die Ausstellung

exit (building) der Ausgang

   (motorway) die Ausfahrt

to expect erwarten

expensive teuer

to explain erklären

extra zusätzlich

eye das Auge

F

face das Gesicht

factory die Fabrik

faint (feeling) schwach

fair (funfair) der Jahrmarkt

to fall fallen

family die Familie

famous berühmt

fan belt der Keilriemen

far weit

fare der Fahrpreis

farm der Bauernhof

fashionable modisch

fast schnell

fat (on food) das Fett

   fat dick

father der Vater

favourite Lieblings-

fawcet der Wasserhahn

fax das Fax

   fax machine das Faxgerät

   to fax faxen/ein Telefax schicken

I feel... ich fühle mich...

ferry die Fähre

to fetch holen

fever das Fieber

a few ein paar

fiancé(e) der (die) Verlobte

field das Feld

to fill füllen

   to fill in (form) ausfüllen

filling (tooth) die Plombe

film der Film

to find finden

fine (money) die Geldstrafe

   (OK) gut/OK

finger der Finger

fire das Feuer, der Brand

fire brigade die Feuerwehr

firm (company) die Firma

first erster

first-aid kit der Verbandkasten

first name der Vorname

fish der Fisch

fishing das Angeln

fishing permit der Angelschein

fishing tackle das Angelzeug

to fit passen

fizzy mit Kohlensäure

flash (photo) der Blitz

flat (battery) leer

   (apartment) die Wohnung

   (shape) flach

flight der Flug

flight number die Flugnummer

floor (storey) der Stock

florist das Blumengeschäft

flour das Mehl

flower die Blume

flu die Grippe

fly (insect) die Fliege

to fly fliegen

fog der Nebel

food das Essen

food poisoning die Lebensmittelvergiftung

foot der Fuß

  on foot zu Fuß

football der Fußball

footpath der Fußweg

for für

  (+ past time) seit

  (+ future time) für

foreigner der (die) Ausländer(in)

forest der Wald

to forget vergessen

fork die Gabel

form das Formular

fortnight zwei Wochen

fountain der Brunnen

fracture der Bruch

France Frankreich

free kostenlos

freezer der Gefrierschrank

to freeze frieren

French (adj) französisch

fresh frisch

friend der (die) Freund(in)

friendly freundlich

from von, aus

in front of vor

fruit das Obst

fruit juice der Fruchtsaft

to fry braten

full voll

  I'm full Ich bin satt

  full board die Vollpension

  full up (hotel) belegt

funny komisch

furniture die Möbel

fuse die Sicherung

G

game das Spiel

garage (repairs) die Werkstatt

garden der Garten

gas das Gas

gate das Tor

gay (homosexual) schwul

gear der Gang

gear box das Getriebe

genuine echt

German (adj) deutsch

  (noun) der/die Deutsche

  (lang) Deutsch

Germany Deutschland

to get (become) werden

  (fetch) holen

  (obtain) bekommen

  (train) nehmen

  to get on (bus) einsteigen

to get off (bus) aussteigen
to get to kommen nach/zu
to get to know kennen lernen
to get up aufstehen
girl das Mädchen
girlfriend die Freundin
to give geben
glass das Glas
glasses die Brille
gloves die Handschuhe
glue der Klebstoff
to go gehen, fahren
to go out ausgehen
gold das Gold
golf das Golf
golf course der Golfplatz
good gut
good-bye (in person)
                Auf Wiedersehen
        (phone)
                Auf Wiederhören
grass das Gras
greasy fettig
Great Britain Großbritannien
green grün
greengrocer's
        die Gemüsehandlung
grey grau
grocer's
        das Lebensmittelgeschäft
ground floor das Erdgeschoss
group die Gruppe
guarantee die Garantie

guide der Führer/die Führerin
guide book der Reiseführer
guitar die Gitarre
gum (teeth) das Zahnfleisch

H

hair die Haare
hairbrush die Haarbürste
hairdresser's der Friseur
hairdryer der Föhn
half die Hälfte, halb
half board die Halbpension
half price zum halben Preis
hand die Hand
hand luggage das Handgepäck
handbag die Handtasche
handkerchief das Taschentuch
happy glücklich
harbour der Hafen
hard (surface) hart
hat der Hut
to have haben
hay fever der Heuschnupfen
he er
head der Kopf
headache Kopfschmerzen
headlights die Scheinwerfer
healthy gesund
to hear hören
heart das Herz
heart attack der Herzinfarkt
heating die Heizung
heavy schwer

heel (shoe) der Absatz
hello! hallo!/Guten Tag
to help helfen
  help! Hilfe!
her sie/ihr
here hier
high hoch
hill der Berg, der Hügel
to hire mieten
his/him sein/ihn/ihm
history die Geschichte
to hitchhike trampen
HIV positive HIV-positiv
to hold halten
hole das Loch
holidays der Urlaub
  (public) der Feiertag
at home zu Hause
(back) home (travel) nach Hause
home address der Wohnort
honest ehrlich
hood (car) die Motorhaube
horn (car) die Hupe
horrible schrecklich
horse das Pferd
horse-riding das Pferdereiten
hospital das Krankenhaus
hot heiß
hotel das Hotel
hour die Stunde
how? wie?
how about...? wie wäre es mit...?
how far? wie weit?

how many? wie viele?
how much? wie viel?
hunger der Hunger
I'm hungry ich habe Hunger
hurry up! beeilen Sie sich!
it hurts es tut weh
husband der Mann

I
I ich
ice das Eis
ice-cream das Eis
ice-rink das Eisstadion
ice-skating das Eislaufen
ill krank
immediate(ly) sofort
important wichtig
impossible unmöglich
in in
including inbegriffen
indicator (car) der Blinker
indigestion
        die Magenverstimmung
infection die Infektion
information die Auskunft
information office
        das Informationsbüro
injection die Spritze
injured verletzt
injury die Verletzung
insect repellent
        der Insektenschutz
inside drinnen
instead (of that) statt(dessen)

insurance die Versicherung
interesting interessant
international international
internet das Internet
interpreter der (die) Dolmetscher(in)
to introduce vorstellen
invitation die Einladung
to invite einladen
Ireland Irland
to iron bügeln
is: he/she/it is er/sie/es ist
island die Insel
it es
Italian (adj) italienisch
Italy Italien

J

jacket die Jacke
jam die Marmelade
to jam (get stuck) klemmen
jar das Glas
jersey der Pullover
jeweller's der Juwelier
jewellery der Schmuck
job die Arbeit
to go jogging joggen gehen
joke der Witz
journey die Reise
juice der Saft
just (only) nur

K

to keep behalten

key der Schlüssel
kind nett, freundlich
kitchen die Küche
knee das Knie
knife das Messer
to knock klopfen
to know (about) wissen
   (person, place) kennen
   I (don't) know Ich weiß (nicht)

L

label das Etikett
lady die Dame/die Frau
lake der See
land das Land
to land landen
landscape die Landschaft
language die Sprache
large groß
last letzte
to last dauern
   at last! endlich
late spät
to laugh lachen
launderette der Waschsalon
laxative das Abführmittel
lead-free bleifrei
to learn lernen
at least mindestens
leather das Leder
to leave (something) lassen
   (depart) abfahren
to leave luggage
   das Gepäck einstellen

left linke
  to the left links
leg das Bein
lemonade die Limonade
length die Länge
less weniger
letter der Brief
library die Bibliothek
licence die Erlaubnis
  (driving) der Führerschein
to lie down sich hinlegen
life belt der Rettungsring
lift der Fahrstuhl/Aufzug
light (colour) hell
  (not heavy) leicht
  (lamp) die Lampe
light bulb die Birne
like (similar) ähnlich
  I like… …gefällt mir
           ich mag…
  it's like… es ist wie…
like this so
line die Linie
lip die Lippe
lipsalve die Lippensalbe
lipstick der Lippenstift
to listen hören
litre der/das Liter
litter der Abfall
little klein
(a) little ein wenig
to live wohnen
loaf (of bread) das Brot

local aus der Gegend
long lang
to look sehen
  to look for suchen
  to have a look (in shop)
                      sich umsehen
loose (clothes) weit
       (screw) locker
to lose verlieren
to get lost sich verirren
lost property office
                      das Fundbüro
a lot (of) viel/viele
loud laut
lounge (hotel) die Lounge
       (house) das Wohnzimmer
to love lieben
lovely schön
low niedrig
luck: good luck! viel Glück!
luggage das Gepäck
luggage trolley der Kofferkuli
lunch das Mittagessen

M

machine die Maschine
made of aus
magazine die Zeitschrift
mail die Post
main Haupt-
to make machen
man der Mann
manager der Manager
many viele

map (of country) die Karte
   (of town) der Stadtplan
market der Markt
married verheiratet
mass (church) die Messe
match (game) der Wettkampf
   (lighter) das Streichholz
matter: it doesn't matter
              es macht nichts
mattress die Matratze
material der Stoff
may I? kann ich?
meal das Essen
mean: what does ... mean?
            Was bedeutet ...?
to measure Maß nehmen
meat das Fleisch
mechanic der Mechaniker
medical ärztlich
medical certificate
         der Krankenschein
medical insurance
         die Krankenkasse
medicine das Medikament
medium-sized mittelgroß
to meet treffen
member das Mitglied
to mend flicken, reparieren
menu die Speisekarte
message die Nachricht
middle die Mitte
migraine die Migräne
milk die Milch
mine: it's mine es gehört mir

mineral water
         das Mineralwasser
minute die Minute
mirror der Spiegel
to miss (train) verpassen
mistake der Fehler
mixed gemischt
mobile phone das Handy
modern modern
moment der Augenblick
money das Geld
month der Monat
monument das Denkmal
more mehr
morning der Morgen
most(ly) meist(ens)
mother die Mutter
motor boat das Motorboot
motorbike das Motorrad
motorway die Autobahn
mountain der Berg
mountaineering das Bergsteigen
moustache der Schnurrbart
mouth der Mund
to move bewegen
Mr Herr
Mrs/Ms Frau
much viel
muscle der Muskel
museum das Museum
music die Musik
must: I must ich muss
my mein

N

nail der Nagel

nail clippers die Nagelzange

nail polish der Nagellack

name der Name

napkin die Serviette

nappy die Windel

narrow eng

nationality die Nationalität

near nah

  near here hier in der Nähe

nearest nächste

neck der Hals

to need brauchen

there's no need

            das ist nicht nötig

needle die Nadel

neither of them

        keiner von beiden

neither … nor … weder… noch …

Netherlands die Niederlande

never nie

new neu

news die Nachrichten

newsagent's der Zeitungsladen

newspaper die Zeitung

New Zealand Neuseeland

next nächste

  next time nächstes Mal

  next to neben

nice (thing) nett/schön

  (person) sympathisch

night die Nacht

night club das Nachtlokal

no nein

I've no idea

        Ich habe keine Ahnung

noisy laut

non-alcoholic alkoholfrei

none keine

non-smoker der Nichtraucher

normally normalerweise

north der Norden/(adj) nördlich

Norway Norwegen

nose die Nase

nosebleed das Nasenbluten

not nicht

not yet noch nicht

nothing nichts

now jetzt

number (of house, etc)

           die Nummer

    (quantity) der Zahl

number plate

      das Nummernschild

nurse die Krankenschwester

nut (fruit) die Nuss

O

occupied besetzt

of von

office das Büro

often oft

oil das Öl

ointment die Salbe

old alt

on an, auf

once einmal

one-way street
die Einbahnstraße

one-way (ticket) einfach

only nur

open offen

to open öffnen

opening times (shops, museums)
Öffnungszeiten

(business) Geschäftszeiten

opera die Oper

opposite gegenüber

optician der Optiker

or oder

orchestra das Orchester

to order bestellen

other andere

our unser

out: he's out er ist nicht da

out of order außer Betrieb

outside draußen

over über

over there da drüben

to overtake überholen

P

to pack einpacken

packet die Schachtel

page die Seite

pain der Schmerz

painkiller das Schmerzmittel

paint die Farbe

to paint malen

painting das Bild

pair das Paar

pale blass

palace der Palast/das Schloss

paper das Papier

paperback das Taschenbuch

parcel das Paket

pardon? wie bitte?

parents die Eltern

park der Park

to park parken

parking disc die Parkscheibe

parking meter die Parkuhr

party die Party

pass der Pass

passenger
der Fahrgast/der Passagier

passport der Pass

pastry das Gebäck

patient der (die) Patient(in)

to pay (be)zahlen

pedestrian der Fußgänger

pen (ball-point) der Kuli

(fountain) der Füller

pencil der Bleistift

penfriend
der (die) Brieffreund(in)

penicillin das Penizillin

pensioner der (die) Rentner(in)

people die Leute

per pro

performance die Aufführung

perfume das Parfüm

period pains
Menstruationsschmerzen

permit die Genehmigung

perhaps vielleicht

personal persönlich

petrol das Benzin

petrol station die Tankstelle

phone das Telefon

to phone anrufen

phone box die Telefonzelle

phonecard die Telefonkarte

phone number die Telefonnummer

photo das Foto

photocopy die Fotokopie

to photograph fotografieren

phrasebook der Sprachführer

to pick someone up abholen

pickpocket der Taschendieb

picnic das Picknick

picture das Bild

piece das Stück

pill die Pille, die Tablette

pink rosa

pipe die Pfeife

place der Ort

place of birth der Geburtsort

places of interest die Sehenswürdigkeiten

plan der Plan

to plan planen

plane das Flugzeug

plaster (sticking) das Pflaster

plastic das Plastik

plastic bag die Plastiktüte

plate der Teller

platform (station) der Bahnsteig/das Gleis

play (theatre) das Stück

to play spielen

please bitte

plug (electric) der Stecker

(sink) der Stöpsel

pocket die Tasche

to point zeigen

poison das Gift

poisoning die Vergiftung

police die Polizei

police station das Polizeirevier

police (wo)man der (die) Polizist(in)

port der Hafen

portable tragbar

porter der Gepäckträger

portion die Portion

possible/possibly möglich

possibly vielleicht

post die Post

to post aufgeben

post office die Post

postbox der Briefkasten

postcard die Postkarte, die Ansichtskarte

poster das Poster

pound (money/weight) das Pfund

powder der Puder

to prefer/I prefer Ich mag lieber

pregnant schwanger
prescription das Rezept
present das Geschenk
pretty hübsch
price der Preis
private privat
probably wahrscheinlich
problem das Problem
processing (film) die Entwicklung
profession der Beruf
programme das Programm
pub das Lokal/die Wirtschaft
public öffentlich
to pull ziehen
pullover der Pullover
puncture das Loch
punctual pünktlich
purse das Portemonnaie
to push (button) drücken
     (car) schieben
pushchair der Kinderwagen
to put stellen, legen
pyjamas der Schlafanzug

Q

quality die Qualität
question die Frage
to queue Schlange stehen
quick(ly) schnell
quiet ruhig
quite (fairly) ziemlich
     (completely) ganz

R

radiator (car) der Kühler
     (room) der Heizkörper
radio das Radio
by rail mit der Bahn
to rain regnen
raincoat der Regenmantel
rash (medical) der Ausschlag
to read lesen
ready fertig
real echt
rear hinten/Hinter-
receipt die Quittung
receive bekommen
receptionist der Empfangschef
to recommend empfehlen
red rot
refill (pen) die Ersatzmine
refreshments die Erfrischungen
to give a refund
     das Geld zurückgeben
region die Gegend
registration form
     das Anmeldeformular
relative der/die Verwandte
relax sich entspannen
religion die Religion
to rent mieten
repair die Reparatur
to repair reparieren
to repeat wiederholen
to reserve reservieren

restaurant
  das Restaurant/die Gaststätte
return ticket hin und zurück
to return (give) zurückgeben
      (travel) zurückfahren
reverse charge call
          das R-Gespräch
to the right rechts
right (correct) richtig
ring der Ring
to ring (doorbell) klingeln
  (phone someone) anrufen
ripe reif
river der Fluss
road die Straße
road sign das Verkehrsschild
romantic romantisch
room das Zimmer
  (space) der Platz
room service der Zimmerservice
rope das Seil
round rund
route die Strecke
rowing boat das Ruderboot
rubber (material) der Gummi
rubbish der Abfall, der Müll
rucksack der Rucksack
ruins die Ruinen
ruler (measure) das Lineal
to run laufen

S
sad traurig
safe ungefährlich
  (strongbox) der Safe
safety pin die Sicherheitsnadel
to sail segeln
sale der Schlussverkauf
for sale zu verkaufen
same: the same das Gleiche
same again, please
    noch einmal das Gleiche, bitte
saucepan der Kochtopf
sausage die Wurst
to say sagen
  What did you say? Wie, bitte?
  How do you say …?
              Wie sagt man …?
scarf der Schal
school die Schule
science die Naturwissenschaften
scissors die Schere
Scotland Schottland
screwdriver der Schraubenzieher
sea die See
seat der Platz
seat belt der Sicherheitsgurt
second (time) die Sekunde
second-hand
          gebraucht, antiquarisch
to see sehen
to sell verkaufen
sellotape der Tesafilm
to send schicken

separate(ly) getrennt
service (church)
     der Gottesdienst
    (restaurant)
     die Bedienung
services (motorway)
     die Raststätte
to sew nähen
shampoo das Shampoo
sharp scharf
to shave sich rasieren
shaver der Rasierapparat
shaving cream die Rasiercreme
she sie
ship das Schiff
shirt das Hemd
shoe der Schuh
  shoelace der Schnürsenkel
  shoe polish die Schuhcreme
  shoe repairer's
     der Schuh-Reparaturdienst
shop das Geschäft, der Laden
to go shopping einkaufen gehen
shop window das Schaufenster
shopping centre
     das Einkaufszentrum
short kurz
shorts die Shorts
shoulder die Schulter
to show zeigen
shower (bath) die Dusche
    (rain) der Schauer
shower gel das Duschgel
shut geschlossen

to shut schließen
shutter (window)
     der Fensterladen
sick (ill) krank
 sickness (illness) die Krankheit
sick: I feel sick mir ist übel
I've been sick
     ich habe mich übergeben
side die Seite
sightseeing die Besichtigung
sights die Sehenswürdigkeiten
sign das Schild
to sign unterschreiben
signature die Unterschrift
silk die Seide
silver das Silber
simple einfach
since seit
to sing singen
single (ticket) einfach
    (unmarried) ledig
single room das Einzelzimmer
sister die Schwester
size (clothes) die Größe
   (shoes) die Nummer
skates Schlittschuhe
to skate Eis laufen
skating rink die Eisbahn
skis Skier
to ski Ski laufen
ski binding die Skibindung
ski-boot der Skistiefel
ski-lift der Skilift

skin die Haut
skirt der Rock
sky der Himmel
to sleep schlafen
sleeping bag der Schlafsack
sleeping car der Schlafwagen
slice die Scheibe
slippers Hausschuhe
slow(ly) langsam
small klein
to smoke rauchen
smoker der Raucher
snack der Imbiss
snow der Schnee
to snow schneien
soap die Seife
socks die Socken
socket (electric) die Steckdose
soft weich
soft drink ein alkoholfreies Getränk
sole (shoe) die Sohle
some (pl) einige
someone jemand
something (else) etwas (anderes)
sometimes manchmal
son der Sohn
song das Lied/der Song
soon bald
I'm sorry Entschuldigung
sour sauer
south der Süden/(adj) südlich
souvenir das Andenken

Spain Spanien
Spanish spanisch
spanner der Schraubenschlüssel
spare part das Ersatzteil
spare tyre der Ersatzreifen
spark plug die Zündkerze
to speak sprechen
special offer das Sonderangebot
speciality die Spezialität
spectator der Zuschauer
speed die Geschwindigkeit
to spell buchstabieren
to spend (money) ausgeben
           (time) verbringen
spoon der Löffel
sport der Sport
square (shape) viereckig
        (in town) der Platz
stadium das Stadion
stain der Fleck
stairs die Treppe
stalls (theatre) das Parkett
stamp (postage) die Briefmarke
to start beginnen
       (car) anspringen
station (rail) der Bahnhof
        (tube) die Station
to stay (on holiday) wohnen
        (remain) bleiben
to steal stehlen
steering wheel das Lenkrad
sting der Stich
stockings die Strümpfe

stolen gestohlen

stomach der Magen

stop (bus) die Haltestelle

stop! halt!

to stop (halt) halten

(doing) aufhören

storm das Unwetter

straight direkt/gerade

straight on geradeaus

street die Straße

street map der Stadtplan

string der Bindfaden

strong stark

student der (die) Student(in)

to study studieren

stupid dumm

sugar der Zucker

suit (clothes) der Anzug

suitcase der Koffer

sun die Sonne

to sunbathe in der Sonne liegen

sunburn der Sonnenbrand

sunglasses die Sonnenbrille

sunny: it's sunny es ist sonnig

sunshade der Sonnenschirm

sun-tan cream das Sonnenöl

supermarket der Supermarkt

supper (evening meal)
das Abendessen

surcharge der Zuschlag

surname der Nachname

to swallow schlucken

Sweden Schweden

sweet (flavour) süß

sweets die Bonbons

to swim schwimmen

swimming pool
das Schwimmbad

(indoor) das Hallenbad

(outdoor) das Freibad

swimming trunks die Badehose

swimsuit der Badeanzug

Swiss (adj) schweizerisch

switch der Schalter

Switzerland die Schweiz

swollen geschwollen

synagogue die Synagoge

T

table der Tisch

to take nehmen

(time) dauern

take-away (food)
zum Mitnehmen

take off der Abflug

to talk sprechen, reden

tall groß

tampon der Tampon

tap der Hahn

taxi das Taxi

taxi rank der Taxistand

tea der Tee

tea bag der Teebeutel

teaspoon der Teelöffel

technology die Technik

television der Fernseher

to tell sagen

temperature die Temperatur
  (fever) das Fieber
temporary provisorisch
tent das Zelt
tent peg der Hering
tent pole die Zeltstange
tennis das Tennis
tennis court der Tennisplatz
tennis racket der Tennisschläger
terminus die Endstation
terrible schrecklich
to text simsen/texten
than als
thank you danke
that (one) der/die/das
the der/die/das
theatre das Theater
their ihr
then dann
there dort
there is/there are es gibt
thermometer das Thermometer
these diese
they sie
thick dick
thief der Dieb
thin dünn
to think (opinion) meinen
  I think so Ich glaube schon
  I'll think about it
         Ich überlege es mir
I'm thirsty Ich habe Durst
this (one) dieser/diese/dieses

this is ... das ist ...
throat der Hals
  throat pastille
        die Halspastille
through durch
thumb der Daumen
thunderstorm das Gewitter
ticket (bus) der Fahrschein
      (plane) die Flugkarte
      (rail) die Fahrkarte
      (entrance)
    die (Eintritts) Karte
  (dry cleaner's) der Zettel
ticket office
    der Fahrkartenschalter
tide (high) die Flut
    (low) die Ebbe
tie die Krawatte
tight eng
tights die Strumpfhose
till die Kasse
time (measure) die Zeit
    (occasion) das Mal
next time nächstes Mal
on time pünktlich
timetable der Fahrplan
tin (can) die Dose
tin opener der Dosenöffner
tired müde
tissues Papiertücher
to (town, country) nach
  (building, road) zu
tobacco der Tabak
tobacconist's der Tabakladen

today heute
toe die Zehe
together zusammen
toilet die Toilette
toilet paper das Toilettenpapier
toiletries die Toilettenartikel
toll die Gebühr, die Maut
tomorrow morgen
tomorrow morning morgen früh
tongue die Zunge
tonight heute Abend
too (much) zu
   (also) auch
tooth der Zahn
   toothache die Zahnschmerzen
   toothbrush die Zahnbürste
   toothpaste die Zahnpasta
torch die Taschenlampe
to touch berühren
tour
   die Rundfahrt, der Rundgang
tourist der Tourist
tourist office das
   Fremdenverkehrsbüro/
   das Informationsbüro
to tow abschleppen
towards gegen
towel das Handtuch
tower der Turm
town die Stadt
town centre die Innenstadt
toy das Spielzeug
traffic (road) der Verkehr

traffic jam der Stau
traffic light die Ampel
trailer der Anhänger
train der Zug
   by train mit der Bahn
transfer (bank) die Überweisung
to translate übersetzen
to travel reisen
travel agent das Reisebüro
travel sickness
                die Reisekrankheit
traveller's cheque der Reisescheck
tree der Baum
trip (excursion) der Ausflug
trousers die Hose
true wahr
   that's true das stimmt
trunk (car) der Kofferraum
to try (attempt) versuchen
       (sample) probieren
to try on anprobieren
tube die Tube
twice zweimal
twin beds zwei Einzelbetten
to type tippen
tyre der Reifen

U

umbrella der Regenschirm
uncle der Onkel
unconscious bewusstlos
under unter
underground die U-Bahn

underpants die Unterhose
to understand verstehen
underwear die Unterwäsche
United States
       die Vereinigten Staaten
university die Universität
until bis
unusual ungewöhnlich
up hinauf
upset stomach
       die Magenverstimmung
upstairs oben
urgent dringend
to use benutzen
useful nützlich
usual gewöhnlich

V

vacancy ein freies Zimmer
  'no vacancies' 'belegt'
vacant frei
vacuum cleaner der Staubsauger
valley das Tal
VAT MwSt (Mehrwertsteuer)
vegetables das Gemüse
vegetarian vegetarisch
very sehr
video cassette die Videocassette
video recorder
       der Videorecorder
view die Aussicht
village das Dorf
vineyard der Weinberg
visit der Besuch

to visit besuchen
visitor der/die Besucher/in

W

to wait warten
waiter der Kellner/Herr Ober!
waiting room der Wartesaal
waitress
       die Kellnerin/Bedienung!
Wales Wales
to go for a walk
       einen Spaziergang machen
to walk zu Fuß gehen
walking (hiking) das Wandern
wallet die Brieftasche
to want wollen
to wash sich waschen
wash basin das Waschbecken
washing powder
       das Waschpulver
washing-up liquid das Spülmittel
wasp die Wespe
watch (clock) die Armbanduhr
to watch sehen
water das Wasser
waterfall der Wasserfall
waterproof wasserdicht
waterskiing das Wasserskilaufen
we wir
to wear tragen
weather das Wetter
weather forecast
       der Wetterbericht
website die Webseite

week die Woche
weekend das Wochenende
well (feeling) gut
    (healthy) wohl
    (water) der Brunnen
west der Westen/(adj) westlich
wet nass
what? was?
wheel das Rad
wheelchair der Rollstuhl
when? wann?
where? wo?
which?
        welcher/welche/welches?
white weiß
who? wer?
whole ganz
why? warum?
wide breit
wife die Frau
wind der Wind
window das Fenster
windscreen
        die Windschutzscheibe
windscreen wiper
                der Scheibenwischer
windsurfing das Windsurfen
wine der Wein
with mit
without ohne
woman die Dame/die Frau
wonderful wunderbar

wood (forest) der Wald
    (material) das Holz
wool die Wolle
word das Wort
to work (job) arbeiten
        (function) funktionieren
worse schlechter
to wrap einpacken
wrist das Handgelenk
to write schreiben
writing paper das Schreibpapier
wrong falsch

Y
year das Jahr
yellow gelb
yes ja
yesterday gestern
yet: not yet noch nicht
you du (F)/Sie (P)
young jung
your dein (F)/Ihr (P)
youth hostel die Jugendherberge

Z
zip der Reißverschluss
zoo der Zoo

When you get back from your trip, try these **teach yourself** titles, available from all good bookshops and on-line retailers:

- **Teach Yourself One-Day German**, by Elisabeth Smith
  Only 50 words and phrases to learn with a 75-minute audio CD and an 8-page booklet. Join Lis and another passenger on their flight to Germany and listen in to the 'One-Day German Challenge'!

- **Teach Yourself Instant German**, by Elisabeth Smith
  Learn German in 6 weeks, on a daily diet of 35 minutes. There's a book with audio support on CD or cassette.

- **Teach Yourself Beginner's German**, by Rosi McNab
  A lively course with lots of real-life situations, dialogues, maps and cartoons. Book with audio support on CD or cassette.